FEAR

ISSUES OF EMOTIONAL LIVING

IN AN AGE OF STRESS

FOR CLERGY AND RELIGIOUS

FORMATION LIBRARY

DAUGHTERS OF ST. PAUL

BOSTON

FEAR

ISSUES OF EMOTIONAL LIVING
IN AN AGE OF STRESS
FOR CLERGY AND RELIGIOUS

THE ELEVENTH
PSYCHOTHEOLOGICAL SYMPOSIUM

J. WILLIAM HUBER

H. RUSSELL SEARIGHT

G. MARTIN KELLER

GILBERT SKIDMORE

MARTIN C. HELLDORFER

AUDREY E. CAMPBELL

JOSEPH L. HART

DAVID E. DOIRON

BRENDAN P. RIORDAN

MARTEL BRYANT

BERNARD J. BUSH

MARIE KRAUS

EDITED BY MARIE KRAUS

AFFIRMATION BOOKS
WHITINSVILLE, MASSACHUSETTS

To
present and former residents
of the House of Affirmation
with love and gratitude

First Edition
© 1986 by House of Affirmation, Inc.

Library of Congress Cataloging in Publication Data

Psychotheological Symposium (11th : 1985 : Boston, Mass., etc.)
    Fear: issues of emotional living in an age of stress for clergy and religious.

    1. Monastic and religious life—Psychology—Congresses. 2. Catholic Church—Clergy—Psychology—Congresses. 3. Fear—Religious aspects—Christianity—Congresses. I. Huber, J. William. II. Kraus, Marie. III. Title.
BX2435.P74 1985   248.8'9   86-3533
ISBN 0-89571-028-5

BF575
· F2
P74
1986

Printed by
Mercantile Printing Company, Worcester, Massachusetts
United States of America

CONTENTS

Foreword

Our fear of love is the most disabling of all fears, and is the greatest impediment to the fullness of life. In our House of Affirmation therapeutic communities, we often encounter people who come to us overwhelmed with fear because of the devastating lack of love in their lives. By establishing trust in relationships with others and self, these same men and women often begin to know and feel for the first time that faith in Christ promises liberation from unreasonable fear. Jesus is the joy of our lives.

The Christian community that works to eradicate fear in the social, economic, psychological, and spiritual spheres of life is responding to Jesus in the glory of his resurrection when he said, "It is I. Do not be afraid."

Sister Marie Kraus, S.N.D.deN., editor of this book, has gathered a collection of essays that will not only challenge our thought but encourage our faith. Affirmation Books is proud to have as the editor of this volume on fear a person as dedicated as Sister Marie to the contemporary media, in particular to the Christian press.

Thomas A. Kane, Ph.D., D.P.S.
Priest, Diocese of Worcester
Publisher, Affirmation Books
Boston, Massachusetts

12 February 1986
Ash Wednesday

Preface

In a world haunted by the threat of nuclear destruction, the topic of fear is certainly an appropriate one. Small children suffer psychologically from the instability and pessimistic tone of the adults around them. Improved communication and the visual impact of television impress on us the dangers and horrors of the world around us: earthquakes, tornadoes, terrorist attacks, travel accidents. We live in an age where we are all touched by fear and anxiety.

So it is not surprising that the eleventh annual House of Affirmation symposium examined the topic of fear. This present volume, *Fear: Issues of Emotional Living in an Age of Stress for Clergy and Religious,* offers the thoughtful essays presented at the symposium by House of Affirmation staff members. They explore the topic from a variety of viewpoints, offering reflections on our fear of God, of the opinion of others, of failure, of intimacy and growth, of aging and retirement, of relating our shameful experiences, and even of our gifts. These chapters contain a wealth of material for reflection and discussion for both religious professionals and lay people.

My gratitude goes to the speakers who presented papers at the Boston, Middletown, San Francisco, St. Louis, and St. Petersburg 1985 symposium programs, and to the writers who submitted papers to be included in this book. An equal debt of gratitude is due the many men and women who attended the sessions. Their interest, enthusiasm, and participation enliven the programs and shape succeeding ones.

We are grateful to all who work behind the scenes to insure the success of the symposium. While so many must remain anonymous, the symposium moderators deserve special mention for their personal grace and generous contribution of time to the success of the days: Rev. John Allan Loftus, S.J., Ph.D. (Boston); Brother Martin C. Helldorfer, F.S.C., D.Min. (Middletown); Marie Hofer, Ph.D. (San Francisco); Rev. J. William Huber, Ph.D. (Webster Groves); Rev. Gerald Fath, O.P., D.Min. (St. Petersburg).

We are also grateful to those who extended hospitality for the meetings: the Sisters of St. Joseph at Aquinas Junior College in Newton; the Sisters of Mercy at Mercy High School in Middletown; the Sisters of the Presentation in San Francisco; the staff of St. John's Mercy Hospital in St. Louis; and the staff and congregation of St. Jude's Church in St. Petersburg.

Each year the symposium is part of our annual Affirmation Weekend, when former residents return to House of Affirmation centers to share their growth-filled journeys with the staff members and each other. Their courage, honesty, and perseverance are an inspiration to all of us.

> Marie Kraus, S.N.D.deN.
> House of Affirmation
> Boston, Massachusetts

14 February 1986

Fear: Friend or foe

J. William Huber

The feeling of fear • Avoiding our fears •
Our friendly helper • Masking the fear •
Reversing the process

Reverend J. William Huber, Ph.D., is director of the House of Affirmation in Webster Groves, Missouri. A priest of the diocese of Pueblo, Colorado, Father Huber received his undergraduate education at St. Thomas Seminary in Denver. He completed graduate work in marriage counseling at the University of Detroit, and received his doctorate in clinical psychology from the California School of Professional Psychology in San Diego. Before joining the staff of the House of Affirmation, he was the founding director of the Pueblo Diocesan Office for Family Life. Father Huber also served in various other pastoral and associate pastor positions before undertaking his graduate studies. He is a member of the American Psychological Association, the American Association of Marriage and Family Therapists, and other professional organizations.

Mark Twain's Tom Sawyer and Huckleberry Finn lived exciting lives. For example, when they explored the caves along the Mississippi River, they were frightened of the sights and sounds and darkness they found there. Yet in spite of their fears, they went back again and again to explore the caves some more. Like many youngsters, these storybook characters discovered excitement in their fear, excitement that beckoned them back to experience it again and again.

Most of us have a bit of Tom Sawyer in us. As children, we may have been afraid of the darkness outside, of the sounds in a cave, or of scary monsters hiding under our bed or lurking behind the bedroom door. Fear of the dark is a very common childhood experience.

As we mature and age, the fear of the darkness outside changes into a fear of the darkness within. The darkness within us is more frightening because it is secretive; it is not easily shared with others. When the fear remains external to us, it can more easily be brought to light and seen for what it is. It can be destroyed by the light of reality. But the darkness within hides in a place where no other person has access. Will I succeed in life? Will others like me? Will I pass my exams? Will anyone ask me out to a party? Will the parishioners, or the superior, or the school parents recognize the efforts I make to minister to them? On and on go these internalized questions we fear.

Each of us lives alone in our private interior space, alone in our hopes for life, alone in our fears about those hopes. Each of us forms our private interior spaces very early in life, where we hide our fears to keep them from overwhelming us.

We need only think about the recent devastating earthquake that hit Mexico City, sending thousands of victims into the streets. The experience made millions of Mexicans very sensitive to any activity beneath the earth's crust. The residents of San Francisco experienced a similar reality nearly eighty years ago. Seismologists and geologists warn that the San Andreas fault is due for another shift that could cause a major earthquake. People who live in earthquake-prone areas fear this darkness outside, the unknown external forces of nature that can be unleashed at any moment.

Few areas of the world are safe from these external forces of nature. In mid-America the New Madrid fault with the potential of inflicting great damage and destruction lies near the boot heel of Missouri. Scientists now warn us that a major quake along this fault could be felt from Dallas to Detroit.

What might be your reaction if this moment the floor began to tremble and shake, and the walls of the room sounded as if they were crumbling? What would you feel? What would you do? Would you shout? Would you run? Where would you go? Would you pray? Would you sit quietly as if nothing were happening? How would you feel?

The external fears of an earthquake can save our life if they help us respond to the impending danger. It is not difficult to imagine such fear. Many of us play "home movies" in our minds, imagining what a nuclear attack might be like. The chills go up and down our spine. Earthquakes and nuclear wars are based on possible realities; but the darkness inside, the unknown elements we store away within our person can also stir our imagination and set us on edge.

The apostles were no strangers to fear. We read in the synoptic gospels about a fear-filled boat trip they took. Although Jesus was with them, he seemed distant and indifferent. Matthew, Mark, and Luke all write about the frightening experience. "Without warning a storm broke over the lake," Matthew writes, "so violent that the waves were breaking right over the boat." What did the apostles do? Their fear impelled them to seek Jesus "and they woke him saying, 'Save us, Lord, we are going down!'" (Matt. 8:23-26). Mark indicates that the apostles were so frightened that they tried to make Jesus responsible for their lives. "Master, do you not care? We are going down!" (Mark 4:39).

The feeling of fear

If you have ever been aboard a ship in high waves, you know the feeling. If you have ever been on a crowded freeway at rush hour and the car in front of you has an accident, you know the feeling. If you have ever been airborne on a jumbo jet and the plane hits turbulence and the captain on the intercom informs you that the plane will make an emergency landing, you know the feeling. If in your present assignment, your superior calls you to the office, you know the feeling. If you are married, and have a hard time financially making ends meet, and your doctor confirms the suspicion that you are pregnant, you know the feeling. If the doctor confirms that your biopsy reveals cancer, you know the feeling. The feeling is *fear*.

Fear can be experienced mildly as a slight apprehension, or fear can be a devastating experience. In a recent newspaper advice column, a reader described fear as a suffocating feeling of one's heart bursting or skipping beats. These attacks came three or four times a day, and finally became so serious the victim woke up sweating, screaming, and gasping for air.

I have known priests to undergo similar panic or anxiety attacks at the altar or in the pulpit. The experience is always a frightening one. Sometimes it is debilitating, and the person can no longer function.

We can place fears on a continuum from mild anxiety to terrifying panic and phobias. If the source of the fear is something outside us, we can take appropriate action because it is objectified as a known quantity. However, most experiences of fear, whether mild or incapacitating, come from within us.

A neighbor of mine experiences agoraphobia, fear of open places. His fear limits him to his house and the sidewalk surrounding it. In the past when he attempted to go beyond those narrow confines to a store only a block away, he became so panic-stricken that he had to be hospitalized. Consciously, he fears being caught in a strange place without convenient access to rest rooms. Unconsciously he fears losing control of his surroundings and of his life. This internalized fear of falling apart makes him a sick man. His fears have enslaved him for many years now; they completely control his life.

"Each of us carries within . . . [ourselves the] 'inner child of the past'—a set of feelings and attitudes brought from childhood. . . . You may remember anything—from your mother's dismay over spilled coffee at a church social, to a party dress or a specific punishment. . . ."[1] How we allow these feelings and attitudes to influence us determines whether they will grow into a foe that incapacitates us, or a friend that teaches and helps us through life.

Which of us at some moment of our lives has not feared "going crazy"? It is a fear shared by many. Other common fears are the fear of rejection, of failure, of making a mistake, of meeting people, of hell, of growing old, of death. Franklin Delano Roosevelt in his first Inaugural Address on March 4, 1933 told the American people that "the only thing we have to fear is fear itself."

Centuries earlier, Lucretius (99–55 BC) stated something similar: "For as children tremble and fear everything in the blind darkness, so we in the light sometimes fear what is no more to be feared than the things children in the dark hold in terror and imagine will come true."

One woman told me that ever since childhood she had been afraid of nearly everything from bugs to elevators. "Generally the unknown is my biggest fear," she finally admitted when she was learning how to integrate her fears and make them her friends.

A school athletic director recalled that as a child and adolescent he was afraid to play baseball. He was on the team, but did not want to play because he was afraid to make a mistake during a game. He was injured twice. Instead of feeling sad about the injuries, he felt "great" because he could then be at the games as a member of the team, but not have to worry about playing. He had internalized his injury into a fear of getting hurt again.

Each of us has a tendency to protect ourselves from what we fear. Rather than search to discover what fear can teach us about ourselves, most of us protect ourselves from that information and so are no longer able to recognize what is going on inside our body. For some people depression is more comfortable than fear. They use it to insulate themselves against facing what they fear, against taking charge of their lives. It seems easier for these persons to withdraw from the world than to face it. My neighbor experiences remaining in his self-imposed prison as safer than attempting to venture into a world that seems much more hostile.

Avoiding our fears

"Whenever I feel afraid, I hold my head up high, and whistle a happy tune so no one will suspect I'm afraid." So goes the refrain of a once popular tune. And oh, how we try to keep people from suspecting we are afraid. Most of us whistle a lot!

Others among us try to cope with their fears by seeking anonymity in crowds. Few of us want to stand out and be noticed. We feel safer and less threatened if we can be one of the nameless faces in a crowd on the highway of life.

Did you ever have the experience of being the focus of a community meeting, or a convent meeting, or a parish team meeting? What did you feel when all eyes and discussion centered upon you? Perhaps you felt like running out of the room, or squeezing through the cracks in the floor. Ten to one you wanted the discussion and focus, positive or negative, to move away from you as soon as possible. Few of us want to be the center of attention. Even when we attempt to disappear into a crowd, we are choosing to be alone in our fears, seeking to isolate ourselves. We are afraid that others will discover our real fears, and so the anonymous crowd helps some of us some of the time to hide our fears.

Few people want others to see them cry. Have you noticed how most of us try to cover our face when we cry? Our hands go up to protect our image because we fear that others would not accept our emotions or hurts. Yet, most of us as caring people befriend others during the time of their tears. Somehow, it is all right for others to cry, but we need to give ourselves the same permission.

The more we remain alone, the more we remain isolated; the more we isolate ourselves, the more we fail to communicate with others. The more we fail to communicate with others, the more our fears terrify and paralyze us. We need to speak the unspeakable truth: we need to name our fears.

We may attempt to mask fear by hiding behind activity. The workaholic is a bit like one ant in the ant pile hurrying here and there while trying not to run into other ants on their way to and from the ant pile.

Fear: Our friendly helper

Examine fear more closely. See it for what it can be when it is integrated: a friend. It can mobilize our strength, prepare us to act, even protect us from harm. Fears about the possibility of earthquakes in California and the damage they could cause, have motivated engineers and local governments to build safer buildings and to plan evacuation routes should people be required to flee. The fear aroused by each tremor can protect the person by urging a move into an open area clear of falling debris. In other words, fear can be a friend when it helps us to avoid things that need to be avoided. Or it can be a foe when it does not.

The fear of cancer has led individuals to the early detection and cure of their own cancer. Today the fear of AIDS has led some segments of our population to act more responsibly in their relationships with others, while it has been a foe leading to panic reactions for others. Each of us can react blindly or we can act reflectively. The choice is ours.

Knowing that we are not alone in our fears but share them with others helps us to befriend those fears. Actor Rock Hudson's revelation that he had AIDS helped large groups of people to rally together to address the need for a cure for AIDS. How much better this action than to judge AIDS merely as a punishment for evil committed by an individual. Only by owning our fears, and talking openly about those fears with others can we understand and constructively deal with fear. "Love drives out fear" (I John 4:18). Love is the product of trust in any relationship. It is the result of sharing our fears with a loved one, of making ourselves vulnerable, and of allowing another to see us as we see ourselves.

Masking the fear

When I was working in our Whitinsville center, I had the good fortune to live through the blizzard of 1978. Much has been written about that blizzard: my outstanding experience during that week was the friendliness of the local people. Unable to travel by car, everyone was forced to walk to town to purchase food supplies and other necessities. People got to know their neighbors as they offered to share supplies with one another. Strangers were talking to strangers.

Although I was born and raised in Colorado, I had never been in a blizzard before. Fifty-two inches of snow fell in one twenty-four-hour period, with strong winds that piled sixteen-foot snow drifts in front of my home, several miles from the nearest store. Strangers came plodding through the snow to offer me bread and milk. They had been able to purchase extra for themselves, and seeing me shoveling snow, they wanted to share.

For five days fear bonded strangers to one another. These relationships helped us cope with the common fears of losing electricity, of water freezing in the pipes, or running out of heating oil. Friendship and love enabled New Englanders to cope with one of the century's biggest blizzards for their area. People unmasked their fears of life, of death, of strangers. Those who did not choose to share their fears or had no one with whom to share were in serious trouble. Some of these men and women later broke down emotionally and needed professional help.

By living community, people had no need to hide, or mask, or suppress their fears. They could admit them to one another, and it is normal to fear a threatening blizzard, especially a "nor'easter" in New England. Living through that storm and its aftermath taught me to befriend my own fear of blizzards. Ever since 1978 I do not fear so much the cold blast of winter's storms because I learned I can cope with even a record-setting blizzard.

When we do not befriend our fears, we may fear going crazy. When we do not deal with our fears, we are "sitting ducks" for problems. Sitting ducks experience fear as a real threat to their life!

Reversing the process

To befriend our fear, it is necessary to reverse the process by which we internalized it. We must externalize the fear once again, get it out into the open, and so become childlike, not childish. We will again need to look into the darkness, objectify it, and get the darkness outside ourselves.

How can we do this? By talking about the fear, by naming it, and trusting that others will understand, or at least allow us to talk about our fear. This discussion will help us to integrate the fear and not permit it to control us. If we had parents or guardians who discouraged us from talking about our fears, or who made light of them, this trusting others to care in the here and now may seem like an added burden to us. We will have to make a real act of trust and faith in our fellow humans who can reflect the incarnate love of God back to us.

As children we had only to look under the bed to realize that the feared monster was not there. When that which we fear is exposed to the light, it can be faced for what it really is. But when kept in the dark, unexposed, internalized, it can grow and overwhelm us. Fears may be compared to fungus, which grows in the dark, but when exposed to the light, dries up and disintegrates.

> If I say: "Let the darkness hide me and the light around me be night," even darkness is not dark for you and the night is as clear as the day. (Ps. 139: 23-24)

Some fears may never totally disappear, but we can live with them. By meeting and facing them, we can gain courage and confidence. "No amount of thinking and talking will get you to the point where you can step out of your swamp without fear; you will have to make the first step while [you are] still afraid."[2] For example, if the bishop or provincial calls me or sends me an official-looking letter, I need to examine the queasiness in the pit of my stomach. What am I expecting the letter or phone call to contain? What is it about authority that causes me to stiffen, break into a cold sweat, and anticipate the worst? If we do not seek to learn from the fear, the fear may snare us. If we examine the fear so as to learn something about ourselves, and call the fear by its true name, then we can turn fear into a friend. Fear can teach us who we are and how we can grow and increase in the awareness of life.

Let me emphasize that we must do this while we are still afraid. To name our fear means that if I am afraid of being transferred and I do not want to be, I must admit and face that fact when I get the letter or phone call. Let me look at the reality of the "named" fear. Then I will be able to dispel the fear and to face the reality of my life and the options it offers.

We cannot delay until after the fears are gone, since the only way to lessen them or even rid ourselves of them is to begin to look at the fear while we experience it. When we act this way, we feel more confident and successful in meeting the demands of the moment. Even if the fear does not disappear, and it may never go completely, "meeting the challenge not only makes us feel great, it also gives us the courage to confront other fears in the future."[3]

What is the interpretation?

Fear, like any other feeling, is neither good nor bad, neither right nor wrong. The interpretation we place on many fears makes them negative. Driving down the highway requires a reasonable amount of fear and caution. I would not want to be a passenger with a driver who claims to be without fear. I am likewise uneasy with drivers who are so totally fearful that they fear to maintain the speed limit, fear to pass a slow-moving tractor, or fear to signal a turn before making it, so that they cause traffic to pile up behind them. My fears are not bad or good. They are a reality for me. If I judge these feelings of fear to be wrong, I will not be able to examine from whence they come, and to own the fact that I am afraid, thus learning from the fear and moving beyond it.

Within all of us is that child of the past who attempted to sustain personal integrity, sometimes at a great cost. In the face of family pressures, that child discovered protective measures and strategies to withstand family conflicts. But are these strategies still helpful? Are today's conflicts the same as those of yesterday? Do we need to cling to those childhood protective measures when we are no longer children?

One man told me about his youth in a family with an alcoholic father. He recalled how his father had cut the son's hair at home to save money and the resulting haircut was very uneven. As a result his brothers and sisters took out their frustrations on the father and the family experienced an uproar. The youngster ran away from the house to a nearby pond where he hid in the hope that he would not get his father into trouble with the rest of the family. He unrealistically felt responsible for the uproar. By not being visible, he hoped, as only a little boy can hope, that the family would forget what the father had done to the boy's hair.

Today, this young man is overcoming his fear of being around the family, lest his presence remind others of the hurts of the past. He no longer believes others see him as the "cause" of the family upsets. But he still struggles with his fear. The child lives on in each one of us.

Love can cause us to behave in what appears to others to be strange ways. Love can also permit us to unmask ourselves when we no longer need to hide. We can truly love another by sharing the fears, because the loved one understands and accepts us. We need to hold one another in our trusting words, and to touch each other if our fears are to become meaningful.

Fears can be our friend or our foe. Risking to expose them and to deal honestly with them makes fears a positive force in our lives. The choice is ours.

Endnotes

1. W. Hugh Missildine, M.D., *Your Inner Child of the Past* (New York: Pocket Books, 1982), p. 10.
2. Jordan Paul and Margaret Paul, *Do I Have To Give Up Me To Be Loved By You?* (Minneapolis: Compcare Publications, 1983), p. 160.
3. Ibid., p. 162.

The fear of breaking family rules

H. Russell Searight

Origin and nature of family rules •
Harmful family rules •
Transforming the present into the past •
Taking the risk: Breaking the rules

H. Russell Searight, Ph.D., is a psychotherapist at the House of Affirmation in Webster Groves, Missouri, and serves on the psychology faculty of St. Louis University where he provides clinical instruction in family therapy. Dr. Searight received a bachelor's degree in psychology from Butler University in Indianapolis, Indiana and master's and doctoral degrees in clinical psychology from St. Louis University. He is a member of the American Psychological Association including the divisions for community psychology, clinical neuropsychology, and psychologists interested in religious issues. Dr. Searight has published articles in the areas of family therapy, primary prevention, and mental health policy.

Nearly all of us spent our early developmental years in a family. However, the impact of our family-of-origin on our adult lives, while one of the least frequently recognized influences, is yet one of the most potent forces shaping our daily existence.

Origin and nature of family rules

As children, the family environment is the context in which we learn about the world. Families provide us with rules for making sense out of our experience and serve as standards for evaluating our own feelings, attitudes, and behavior. In their book, *The Family Crucible,* Carl Whitaker and Augustus Napier describe the family as a "miniature society, a social order with its own rules, structure, leadership, language, style of living, zeitgeist. The hidden rules, the private rituals and dances that define every family as a unique microculture may not be easy for an outsider to perceive at first glance, but they are there."[1]

As we grow up and leave our family, that environment stays with us in the form of basic rules. Often these rules mesh very well with the world outside of the family. For example, being thoughtful of others, respecting personal differences, accepting responsibility are values transmitted by our parents that generally serve us well as adults. However, sometimes these rules are the source of tension, anxiety, and depression when they persist into adult life. For those who were raised in families in which the climate was rigid, punitive or harsh, adulthood is likely to center around themes of anticipated retribution and rejection. The fear of breaking these unstated, often unconscious, rules is a powerful force shaping our current behavior.

Although developmentally we have not been a child in a family for many years, we often feel and behave as if we still were. W. Hugh Missildine describes this phenomenon: "Life, as you understand it and live it, was learned in . . . [your family-of-origin]. Whatever its peculiarities, you gained from your family the feeling of being 'at home.' It is this feeling that your inner child of the past still seeks."[2] Some readers may disagree with these statements. "That's not true. I'm not a child. I'm an independent adult and I'm completely in control." Intellectually, they are correct. However, at the emotional level, we sense that some psychological or physical harm will befall us if we violate these unspoken family norms. This fear of breaking family rules is often unconscious, and experienced consciously not as fear but indirectly as anxiety, a sense of being trapped, or a feeling of being controlled by unknown forces.

When we were young children, breaking these family rules typically led to direct punishment. However, as we grew older, we internalized these rules as part of our being. During adolescence, when we developed significant relationships outside of the family, we may have inadvertently violated these norms or in some instances, have begun to question them. Unfortunately, many parents, rather than encourage independent reflection, respond with veiled threats of withdrawal of their affection and support when an adolescent questions the family's shared reality. The fear of losing parental love at a time when the vulnerable young adult is struggling with issues of autonomy, competence, and self-worth is a terrifying prospect. The result is that many adults never succeed in breaking the family rules and establishing their own identity apart from that of their family-of-origin.

Harmful family rules

Listed below are some often unstated yet powerful rules that govern family functioning. It is important to remember that because they are typically unlabeled these rules invoke the fear of being controlled by unknown, almost mysterious, forces:

— Do not express feelings. In particular, do not become angry, sad or express weakness.
— Do not become close to outsiders. If you do, you are betraying the family.
— Enjoying yourself is wrong. You should always be productive.
— Reaching out to others for help means you are weak. Solve your problems on your own.
— Being assertive and taking care of your own psychological needs means you are demanding and selfish. You should accept "your lot in life."
— Sexuality is a taboo topic that nice people do not discuss.
— Anything that goes wrong is your fault and you deserved it.

Transforming the present into the past

Because these rules continue to reside within us, they can transform people and situations of our current life into those of the past.

A middle-aged woman religious says: "Whenever I have a conversation with my superior, I feel like a six-year-old girl. I never ask questions; I only listen to what I'm being told. Intellectually, I recognize these feelings are ridiculous: my superior is not my mother, but this childlike deference takes over whenever I'm with her. I hate to have this happen but I can't control those feelings."

This situation is a common example of how our childhood family patterns are re-created in the present. Persons who were raised in families characterized by chaos, unpredictability, and harshness have an intense fear of violating the internalized family rules. In fact, this experience is one of the most significant paradoxes observed in psychotherapy. As adults, persons who were traumatized by abuse or neglect, whether physical or emotional, frequently cannot tolerate affirmation, caring, and affection from others. They often respond to displays of support with distrust and even terror. To understand this response, it is useful to remember that for those men and women raised in such family environments, being affirmed is a completely new and unexpected experience. Because it is unknown, it is likely to activate considerable anxiety and an ominous sense that the more familiar experience of being rejected, exploited or punished is about to occur at any minute; the feelings of being cared for and valued are simply "too good to last."

A young priest describes this situation in his own life.

I grew up in a family in which all our activities centered around my father's drinking. The only thing that was consistent in our home was unpredictability. My dad was caring, warm, and affectionate when he was sober. Once he started drinking, he'd go on a rampage; he would scream and yell about anything and everything. Sometimes my dad became violent toward my sisters and myself. As an adult, I find that it's hard for me to trust others, particularly those in authority. Even when people are being kind to me, I don't trust them; I feel as if the ax is going to fall at any minute. The longer others treat me with kindness the more fearful I become. I keep saying to myself, "This can't last; it's not the way life really is."

The rules that are communicated to children in families like the one described above often lead to self-punishment. The message is conveyed to the children that they deserve the harshness meted out to them. For example, in alcoholic families, the children are often led to believe that they somehow cause their parent(s) to drink and therefore, also cause the alcoholic's violence. Although this attitude is irrational and a good example of the magical thinking that parents sometimes transmit to children, such feelings of intense personal responsibility for events outside of one's control are carried into adulthood. As adults, these men and women often feel as if they are contaminated and destructive to others. Because they view themselves in this light, they punish themselves through excessive work and denial of leisure activities or through social isolation.

As noted in the above examples, we often project family rules onto the relationship patterns of our adult lives. This projection process can be extremely powerful. By re-enacting our family rules in our adult life, a self-fulfilling prophecy occurs. The other person, be it a religious superior, fellow community member or co-worker, unwittingly participates in the recapitulation of our childhood family experience. Marriages, friendships, work relationships, and vocational choices often represent attempts to re-create the familiar world of our past family life in the present. These forces, although usually not completely conscious, take the form of behavior that re-enacts our relationships with parents and siblings within our current social context. Thus, persons whose internalized family rules center around themes of rejection or punishment will often relate with others so as to bring about these emotionally painful experiences.

A seminary student in therapy describes this process very well.

My father was extremely critical and domineering toward me. I could never do anything right. Even though I've done ok in school I've always felt I'm putting up a front. I see this most in my social life or better put, lack of it. I feel that if people really get to know me, they won't like what they see. As I get closer to someone, I feel as if I can't control myself. I seem to behave *deliberately* so as to make them mad at me; sarcastic comments just keep coming out of my mouth. I'm late for scheduled meetings with them, and I "forget" to return their phone calls. Pretty soon they are so infuriated with me that any sort of friendship we might have had is now beyond repair. When the final blowup occurs, I don't try to defend myself. In fact, I feel a strange sense of relief; the threat that they could really find me out is gone.

I've come to realize that I expect the harsh criticism that I received from my father and I'm very successful in bringing this criticism about. My friends have no idea what's going on; they eventually just get fed up with me for being irresponsible. Intellectually, I can recognize what's happening. Emotionally, I am terrified when I think about behaving differently.

Taking the risk: Breaking the rules

Murray Bowen, a family therapist, has described a developmental process which he terms differentiation. It involves establishing a personal identity separate and unique from our family-of-origin.[3] Persons who are highly differentiated are able to recognize the emotional force of family roles. Through the cognitive process of recognizing and labeling these emotional forces, highly differentiated persons are able to make free choices about their behavior. In contrast, adults who are poorly differentiated are still emotionally fused with their family; they do not have an identity separate from their parents and siblings. These persons, according to Bowen, have very little in the way of personal integrity and lack appropriate interpersonal boundaries. In addition, poorly differentiated persons are at greatest risk for re-creating their family dynamics in their adult lives.

A first step to preventing this recapitulation is to develop a thorough understanding of the way that your family-of-origin functioned. By acquainting yourself with the concept of family rules and reflecting on your upbringing, you can begin to label some of these standards that continue to regulate your adult life. As a therapist, I hear clients say, "I can see that being assertive is an acceptable way of standing up for myself and I understand that it's a healthy way to be, but I still *feel* that it's somehow wrong, bad, and selfish. I can see it up here [pointing to their head] but not down here [pointing to their stomach or heart]." When a client speaks this way, I often ask, "Whose voice do you hear; who says you are bad for taking care of yourself?" Almost automatically, clients will respond, "I hear my mother [or father, or grand-parent]."

Another way that adults are stimulated to reflect upon family rules is through their emotional responses to nonfamily members with whom they interact. When our emotional reaction to another (be it anger, fear, resentment) seems out of proportion, we can ask ourselves which family member the person psychologically resembles. It is possible we are converting our superior, friend, or co-worker into one of these ghosts from our childhood.

By recognizing and labeling these long-held rules as originating in our family, we can begin to obtain true control over our own life as independent adults. Although obvious at the intellectual level, it is often a continual emotional struggle for us to recognize that we are no longer children in a family. The past is *past*. We are *now* in a different place and a different time. These family rules did, indeed, govern our childhood but they do not have to determine our adult life. As children we were often helpless and dependent upon others for our security and well-being; as adults, this is no longer true. We now have the freedom and resources to be a parent to ourselves.[3]

Unfortunately, the process of becoming free from oppressive family rules is not so simple as described here. As the seminarian noted, the recognition that these rules are still operative is only a limited part of the struggle. The strong fear of violating these rules persists. The pervasiveness of this fear can render impotent any intellectual insights about family rules that we may have. This fear appears to stem from our childhood in which breaking family rules, believing and acting differently from parental beliefs and expectations, was met with threats to our most basic source of security, parental love. Even in the most abusive and neglectful households, children maintain a belief that their parents love them. Objectively, it is fairly easy to recognize that as adults, we can be parents to ourselves and that others do care about us. At an emotional level, however, the fear of being helpless persists. Only by taking risks and breaking the oppressive rules of the past can we find that our fears are unfounded. By behaving in ways that violate these harmful rules, by nurturing ourselves, by acting assertively, by reaching out to others, we find that these fears are not grounded in reality. This task is a significant challenge for many. It takes courage to experience and confront fear. But the reward, the psychological freedom of truly being in control of our lives, is worth the struggle.

Endnotes

1. Augustus Y. Napier and Carl A. Whitaker, *The Family Crucible* (New York: Bantam Books, 1978), p. 78.
2. W. Hugh Missildine, M.D., *Your Inner Child of the Past* (New York: Simon and Schuster, 1963), p. 30.
3. Murray Bowen, *Family Therapy in Clinical Practice* (New York: Jason Aronson, 1978), pp. 159-170.

Fear of being one's self

G. Martin Keller

Eternal fears • Internal fears •
Healthy sense of self • Mirroring and idealizing •
Development through relationships •
Experience of emptiness • Community living

Reverend G. Martin Keller, O.S.A., Psy.D., a licensed clinical psychologist, is an assistant director of the House of Affirmation in Whitinsville, Massachusetts. A member of the Order of St. Augustine, he received a master's degree in theology from Augustinian College, Washington, D.C., and a doctoral degree in clinical psychology from Nova University in Florida. Before joining the staff of the House of Affirmation, Father Keller was involved in parochial and campus ministries. For several summers he was a professor of pastoral studies at the Institute for Ministries at Loyola University, New Orleans, Louisiana. Father Keller is a member of the American Psychological Association and a frequent lecturer and workshop facilitator.

A great variety of siutations can cause people to grow fearful. In some cases these fear-producing events may seem bizarre or laughable. For instance, some people are afraid of the number thirteen. Friday the thirteenth will usually provoke some comments in any gathering. In buildings, the thirteenth floor is often omitted and elevators mysteriously pass from the twelfth floor to the one directly above, the fourteenth floor. Some cities lack the thirteenth avenue in a series of numbered streets. Many people find the stir caused by the number thirteen a bit curious if not downright amusing. This is definitely not the case for triskaideckaphobics, a name given to people who are actually afraid of the number thirteen.

External fears

Many persons are also puzzled to understand the fear generated in some people by going through tunnels or crossing over bridges. However, as we name snakes, large spiders, or extreme heights we begin to empathize with those who become very fearful in these presences, because we admit our own discomfort in similar situations. I imagine that most of us could readily sympathize with a claustrophobic, not wanting ourselves to be confined in any cramped space. I remember how I shuddered when I watched on TV a rescue worker in Mexico City after the earthquake, edging into a small opening in the rubble of a hotel, tons of concrete threatening to fall on him and crush him to death.

Certain persons find different parts of the external world not only frightening, but panic-producing. They begin to perspire, grow pale, and tremble. Their eyes widen and they feel immobilized—too panicked to escape, unable even to cry out to vent their extreme fear.

Internal fears

The point I would like to develop in this paper is that just as there are frightful things that inhabit the external world of some persons, there are fearful monsters that prowl about in the internal world of some of us. Here I am not speaking of the wide-eyed, terrorized souls who may be encountered in locked wards of our mental hospitals or the frightened people we see talking to themselves on the streets of large cities. I am referring to the walking wounded: people who are very much like us. They do not do bizarre things; they do not appear frightened or panicked. They do not live under lock and key in mental institutions. They may live in convents and rectories; they may be found teaching, nursing or preaching. They have acquaintances and friends, hold jobs (sometimes quite responsible ones), and live much as normal people do. Yet in their quiet moments, when they are alone and look inside themselves, they grow frightened. Instead of seeing themselves, they find a large empty space, a hole, where they should be. They are confronted by their own inner emptiness. These men and women lack a fully developed self. They do not know where they came from, where they are now or where they are going. They do not know who they are. They have no ambitions or ideals of their own. Instead they are living out the goals and values of their parents, the Church, their spouse, or society in general. If they ever had a self, they feel they never knew it and that now they have lost it. When they reflect on their emptiness, they become very frightened.

Healthy sense of self

In order to make clear the predicament of persons who are experiencing a lack of selfhood I would like to trace the development of a healthy sense of self. This description is based primarily upon the clinical work and theories of the late Heinz Kohut.

How does a person become a person? Let us begin with the infant. The newborn, of course, has no actual personality. Her personality develops in a matrix consisting of her genetic make-up and the environment into which she is born. Just as she needs oxygen and nourishment to develop physically, she needs parents who will provide a psychological milieu in which she can begin to develop her personality or selfhood.

A healthy personality develops through healthy interactions between the infant and the parents, chiefly, in the beginning, the mother. The baby boy raises his arms and gurgles in a smiling fashion. In response the mother smiles, imitates the gurgle, reaches for his arms, and plays the game "so big." The baby cries and shows he is in distress. The mother responds by frowning in a concerned way, recognizing the baby's distress, and then proceeding to soothe the baby by changing his diaper or feeding him. A stranger approaches and the baby cries. The mother in a concerned voice asks, "Did the big man scare you? Oh, yes. Well, he has gone and everything will be all right." The child falls, lightly scraping his knee, and begins to cry. Mother responds in empathic tones, "Oh, my heavens! Did you hurt yourself? Let me see. Oh, look, you scraped your knee. Here, let me put this cold cloth on it." Then she plays the game, "I'll kiss it and make it all better."

Mirroring and idealizing

If we step back and look at the interactions between mother and child we see that the mother is really mirroring the feelings of the child. If the child is joyous, she is joyful; if the child is playful, so is mother; if the child is scared, mother acknowledges the fright. In effect, mother is validating the feelings of her child. She is telling the child: "What you feel is o.k." But the mother is also soothing and reducing the tension of the child's distress. First, however, she acknowledges the distress in an empathic way, and only then tries to make it better. The child learns that tension can be lowered. If he learns that lesson well, over time he will be able to soothe himself and reduce the tension of a distressing situation alone. If he falls and scrapes his knee, he will get up, cry a bit, and then console himself. If he does not learn the lesson, he will escalate his crying into a tantrum, break a vase, kick the dog, or do things to soothe himself other than paying attention to his knee. This child, when under some stress or tension as an adult, will avoid focusing on the cause of the stress. He could easily turn to alcohol, drugs, sex, or some other addictive behavior to reduce the tension he feels.

But I digress—back to the healthy development of the child. Through the mother's mirroring, the child learns to validate her feelings, acknowledge that what she feels is o.k., and continue to grow in self-assertiveness so that she can comfortably express to others what she feels. Alice Miller in her book *Prisoners of Childhood* makes a plea for parents not only to allow, but to encourage small children to express themselves.[1] Too often parents stifle a child's self-expression, much to her detriment in developing a healthy personality.

Besides mirroring which is important throughout life, but especially from birth to age four or five, parents perform another critical function for the healthy development of their child's personality. They serve as idealized persons for the child, especially during the years from five through eight. The son will literally try to walk in his father's shoes. The daughter will get into mom's make-up kit and experiment with lipstick and rouge. Children need to see their parents as perfect and all-knowing and able to make everything better. Parents do well to show their children how smart, strong and talented they are, thereby providing their children with values and ideals to strive toward in later life. The myth of the perfect parents comes crashing down all too soon, especially in teenage years. But it is important for small children to idealize their parents.

Integrating these two parental functions—mirroring and being idealized—the child begins the process of healthy personality development. She acknowledges and accepts her inner thoughts and emotions, develops self-assertiveness to express her inner experience to others, and begins to acquire skills and talents to accomplish and fulfill her values and ideals. This development is a lifelong process. As Kohut states, "The psychologically healthy adult continues to need the mirroring of the self by self-objects . . . and he continues to need targets for his idealization."[2]

Development through relationships

Let us look next at healthy development of the self from the perspective of Carl Rogers. I would like to offer a few observations from his works that highlight the principal factors in healthy self-development: respect, empathy, unconditional positive regard, and what Rogers calls "congruence." As a clinician, Rogers speaks of client-therapist relationships, but we can easily apply his words to other relationships, such as parent-child, teacher-student, and friend-friend.

> Client-centered therapy is very widely applicable . . . indeed in one sense it is applicable to all people. An atmosphere of acceptance and respect, of deep understanding, is a good climate for personal growth, and as such applies to our children, our colleagues, our students, as well as to our clients, whether these be "normal," neurotic, or psychotic.[3]

Rogers next describes the growth-promoting effect of empathy as it occurs in a therapeutic or healing setting.

The counselor says in effect:

> To be of assistance to you I will put aside myself . . . and enter into your world of perception as completely as I am able. I will

become, in a sense, another self for you—an alter ego of your own attitudes and feelings—a safe opportunity for you to discern yourself more clearly, to experience yourself more truly and deeply.[4]

Finally, Rogers speaks of unconditional positive regard and congruence of the self.

> It appears that one of the most potent elements in the relationship is that the therapist "prizes" the whole person of the client. It is the fact that he feels and shows an unconditional positive regard toward the experiences of which the client is frightened or ashamed, as well as toward the experiences with which the client is pleased or satisfied, that seems effective in bringing about change. Gradually the client can feel more acceptance of all of his own experiences, and this makes him again more of a whole or congruent person, able to function effectively.[5]

To summarize then, Rogers is saying that in an atmosphere of respect, genuine understanding, empathy, and unconditional positive regard, men and women will be able to validate their own thoughts, feelings and experiences, discern who they really are, come to self-acceptance and wholeness, and function as complete and effective persons.

Experience of emptiness

Let us now turn our attention to persons who have not developed an identifiable and cohesive sense of self. These are the people who are so frightened by the deficits they see within themselves.

First of all, they experience an inner emptiness, a barrenness of soul. They have not developed an attitude of self-assertiveness, not knowing or being able to validate their own thoughts, emotions or experiences. Instead, the opinions and expectations of others become crucial to them. They seek out ways to please others and to become acceptable to them in place of feeling accepted in their own eyes. They are rootless and easily carried along by prevailing winds, because they lack abiding personal values and ideals.

Others will experience these men and women as empty and life-less, lacking self-motivation. An essential part of them seems to be missing.

Many of them will be addicted to drugs, sex or alcohol in order to feel alive or excited. Or an addiction may be the only way they can soothe themselves and reduce the tensions they experience in day-to-day living.

Some may appear vain, arrogant, self-centered or conceited as they look for mirroring in their relationships or as they search for an antidote to their strong feelings of inferiority.

Some become "nice guys or gals," having cut themselves off from their anger, jealousy, and other so-called negative feelings because they cannot justify these feelings and find them unacceptable.

Finally, some appear lazy and unproductive because they feel they have no skills or talents. They spend most of their time trying to look good, bluffing their way through life, rather than getting down to the hard work of living it.

There are, as you see, many different ways of being for these persons, but the root cause of their difficulties is based on a profound lack of a cohesive, identifiable, acceptable sense of self.

Community living

Finally, I would like to turn our attention to implications for clerical and religious community living in light of the theories of Kohut and Rogers.[6] Kohut has stated that a healthy developing personality continues to need mirroring by others and to find people who can be idealized throughout life. The question is: "Can this happen in religious communities?"

Here I am not suggesting that sisters, brothers, priests or family members become amateur therapists. But I do believe it is possible for us to help establish a therapeutic setting in which healthy living can take place. We can cocreate an environment of acceptance, respect, understanding, and growth.

In some communities, the slogan seems to be: "Keep your head in the trenches." The sense is that if you expose yourself, you will be shot. In such places it is difficult to be a talented person. The scripture is changed to read: "Hide your light under a bushel basket." For example, are people free to display their art work in the community room without being flayed alive by critics? Do priests feel able to preach to their communities during daily Mass, or is the homily a rare occurrence out of fear of reprisals at the breakfast table or a silent undercurrent of rejection? Is it possible to talk about a new idea, an effective teaching strategem, a gratifying experience in ministry, or must the principal topics at breakfast, lunch, and dinner be the weather and the food? At the risk of bragging, one can help create the atmosphere that this community is indeed a group of creative, talented people.

And what of the elderly in the community? Do they sit with vacant eyes and silent tongues or are they driven to sarcasm and complaints? Are their accomplishments and contributions to the history of the community known and acknowledged? Are they encouraged to share their experiences and their wisdom with the younger community members?

Some communities are characterized by an atmosphere of unreal sweetness and light. Never is heard a discouraging word simply because it is not permitted. Instead there are frequent moments of tense silence. Words expressing anger, frustration, complaints, jealousy, and hurt are rarely expressed. In contrast, could we not simply acknowledge that we are indeed frail human beings with our faults, failings, blemishes, and warts, and begin talking about our shadow side feelings about ourselves and our living together? Can we acknowledge and accept the different emotions and perceptions of others without feeling personally threatened or attacked? Can we create an atmosphere where people are encouraged to be themselves and find themselves valued and accepted for being themselves?

My point is that many people, frightened by their lack of selfhood, live in deadening and unproductive ways. We know some of them and in varying degrees we are these people. But our psychological development is never finished. We can continue our own growth and be instruments for the development of others in our roles as teachers, nurses, ministers.

In this presentation, I have tried to highlight the importance of mirroring, idealization, empathy, respect, understanding, self-assertiveness, and unconditional positive regard. These qualities are responsible for our ongoing development. Their continued presence in our lives is necessary if we wish to make our own world and the worlds of others safe and healthy and less frightening places to be.

Endnotes

1. Alice Miller, *Prisoners of Childhood* (New York: Basic Books, 1981).
2. Heinz Kohut, *The Restoration of the Self* (New York: International Universities Press, 1977), p. 188n.
3. Carl Rogers, *Client-centered Therapy* (Boston: Houghton Mifflin, 1951), p. 230.
4. Ibid, p. 35.
5. Carl Rogers, "A theory of therapy, personality, and interpersonal relationships, as developed in the client-centered framework," in S. Koch, ed., *Psychology: A Study of a Science: Vol. 3. Formulations of the person and the social context* (New York: McGraw-Hill, 1959), p. 208.
6. See E. Kahn, "Heinz Kohut and Carl Rogers: A timely comparison," *American Psychologist* 40 (September, 1985): 893-904.

The importance of fear

Gilbert Skidmore

Historical context • Insufficiency of knowledge •
Jesus as role model

Gilbert Skidmore, M.Ed., L.C.S.W., a psychotherapist at the House of Affirmation in Montara, California, received his master's degree in expressive therapies from Lesley College in Cambridge, Massachusetts and is currently pursuing his doctorate at the Professional School of Psychology in San Francisco. In addition to individual and group work, Mr. Skidmore has a keen interest in the problems of community. Using psychodrama as a therapeutic tool, he offers insights to the way we see ourselves in relation to those around us.

We all know what it means to be afraid. Fear begins as soon as we become aware of ourselves as persons in the world. For example, we may remember nightmares as a child, or we may recall seeing our brothers and sisters waking in the middle of the night, terrified of the boogie man. As we grow older these experiences become more real and we move these fears outside of our personal or internal experience into our thoughts and feelings. They start to have a life of their own. We begin to see them in our daily lives. We experience fear through disappointments at work, in relationships, and hurt feelings. We struggle to understand and cope with these fearful experiences. We talk about fear, we try to understand why we are afraid of an experience, we try to find out where our fear came from.

Historical context of fear

Our personal fears are part of a much larger historical context. When the human race came into being, we were not aware of being afraid, but we knew that we needed to survive in order to remain alive. We did this by struggling against the elements in the world and the larger creatures with whom we existed. We did the best we could. Our sense of fear was external and we coped with it day to day. Moving up the evolutionary ladder to civilization as we know it, we came to another phase of development. We started to develop a sense of God, whether it was a personal deity, a symbol, or an abstract representation. We used that initial relationship to cope with the external dangers around us—other animals, other people who were strangers, or physical calamities. We looked for succor and support from our gods. In times of trouble we still do this today, turning to God for help and strength.

Some theorists talk about fear in relation to consciousness (or being aware of ourselves). They hypothesize that consciousness as we know it did not exist until about three thousand years ago. This new way of looking at our own conscious development means that up until 1100 B.C. we were not aware that our actions caused things to happen. We felt we were guided by the spirits or messages from the gods. Today we would call this superstition and would scoff at it. If that is the case, then we are only about 3000 years old consciously. Considering how long we have been on this planet then, we are struggling to comprehend the world from a younger, more adolescent stage rather than from a mature consciousness.

I want to point out this concept because as we look at the problem of fear we are often perplexed. We want answers now but maybe we are just not ready yet. We are still growing and struggling to understand ourselves. Like children we are impatient to reach a conclusion or answer.

I know this dilemma from my own life. I am in the process of getting my doctorate and although I enjoy the work, it can be a horribly frustrating experience for me. As much as I read and try to gain knowledge and understand theories, more often than not I do not find answers. Instead, much of this knowledge and theory conflict and raise more questions than they answer.

Partly because we search for answers to this problem, the twentieth century is considered the age of fear. We find ourselves asking, "What is this phenomenon we confront in our everyday life?"

Psychology struggles with this task in a practical way using principles it learned from its parent, philosophy. Psychotherapy also struggles in a practical way to help people find a sense of meaning. In my own work as a psychotherapist, I turn more and more to philosophy and to religion for answers to the questions of why we exist and why we are here.

Spinoza, a seventeenth-century philosopher, wrote about fear as a subjective problem. He saw it as the state of one's mind—fear juxtaposed with hope. The nineteenth-century philosopher, Kierkegaard, talked about fear as a desire for what one dreads: a sympathetic relationship. It is an alien power which lays hold of an individual. We cannot tear ourselves away, nor have we the will to do so, for we fear what we desire. We need to look into the interrelationship of our emotions and thoughts.

Insufficiency of knowledge

In my work as a psychotherapist, I see more and more that thought rules over feeling. In our everyday lives we question our feelings over our more self-assured sense of what we think. In growing up most of us learned, "I'm not going to pay attention to my feelings; I'm going to pay attention to my thoughts." Recently, however, a stronger interrelationship between our thoughts and our feelings has emerged. As we seek out others in order to push away the loneliness and fear of being alone, we can compare this interrelationship to what's going on inside of us. Rather than compartmentalize our feelings like anger and love, we can understand the relationship between what we think about them and what we feel about them.

It is important for us to acknowledge and understand this tremendous body of experience within us which is our emotions. Whereas in the past we considered feelings as unauthentic, we now need to pay attention to what we feel. I encourage clients to get in touch with what they feel, and then attempt to make some sense of it.

The theologian Reinhold Niebuhr saw fear as a precondition to sin, an internal manifestation of temptation in life. Fear then becomes an exotic fruit. We feel that as it overwhelms us it causes us to do things with which we may be uncomfortable (which I take to mean sin). If we look at that principle in light of thoughts and feelings being in a sympathetic relationship to each other, then our sins are very important to us. Indeed, all experiences are important to us, for they shape what we are to become. Therefore, the anger that we feel is as important as the warm and loving feelings that we have.

If we are afraid, how do we cope? One way we cope with fear is through faith—our relationship with God and how God is present in our lives. Another way is through the insights we gain as we struggle to understand our fears. Theoretically, fear becomes a breach between ourselves and the world around us. In psychotherapy we talk about identification or identity. On a more basic level, we have the sense that we do not belong anymore. A tremendous despair and dread come over us as well as a sense of alienation. An existentialist would say, "If we exist by ourselves, we have no meaning." In order to "be" we must relate to things. In scientific terms, we start to talk about the "object" (ourselves), in relationship to the subjective (people and things around us). Fear overwhelms us when there is a breakdown between ourselves and the world around us.

I experienced this with the unexpected death of my mother twelve years ago. I was in Boston working and building my own life. But I knew where my family was and I could go to them if I needed them. Then suddenly I found out my mother had died. I remember sitting with a few friends of mine overwhelmed with a tremendous sense of dread. Having experienced the death of a loved one for the first time in my life, I did not understand anything anymore. I felt as if I were aboard a boat that had been docked on the shore and then someone untied the rope and I started to drift away.

All the things I had come to know seemed to be in question. That sense of dread or fear is the experience of not feeling connected anymore. An important anchor for me was gone and I was now going to have to make my own sense of things, my own meaning, without my mother's tangible support.

Although we tend to theorize and abstract to find answers, we can also come to a sense of self-awareness by participating in our own experience. Religion expresses this truth in terms of faith. We can use our faith in God to make the step between theory and reality. Psychotherapy also encourages us to become aware of ourselves and our behavior to bridge that gap. Or we can use the essence of our experience to understand what is occurring in the here and now by asking, "Does it have meaning? Is it important? Is it right or wrong? Is this what I want to do?"

As far as we know, out of all the creatures in the world, only humans are aware that they exist. We are the only ones who feel we are here. This sense of existence can bring a feeling of dread which we try to overcome by living inauthentically in the world. We ask, "What do I need to get by? What do I need to do? Do I need to be polite?" Or we say, "I need to go to work; I need to not offend people."

As we assume this particular mantle of living, which we identify from our parents and other people in the world, we become aware that things do not satisfy us. The task of pleasing others is partially fulfilling but it leaves a gap for us—the gap of what we want in the world. All of us experience this tension in trying to meet our own needs while meeting those of the people around us. When we are able to achieve a balance, we feel we are alive. We also feel unafraid.

By contrast, when those things come into question, everything becomes distorted. We question all of ourselves rather than just the here and now momentary experience of distress. We generalize rather than struggle with the moment because we are afraid to look at ourselves at close range, questioning ourselves and what we are doing. Sadly, and perhaps ironically, the more we become aware of ourselves the more we become afraid. In fact, we use this subjective experience to avoid the despair and dread we feel. Earlier I spoke of this as the fear of dying. If we really become aware of ourselves we will know that we will not always be here. We struggle to overcome that fear.

But if we know all this, why don't we manage better? We have all this knowledge, some answers, and yet we still have questions.

Jesus as role model

In our faith we rely on God for help. God helps us find out where we are going, and is there with us. In our day-to-day lives we can also look to Jesus for support. Lately, I have been thinking and feeling more about Jesus and this has put me in touch with some of my own life themes. As a child I saw God as a judge. Often in families our parents use God like a distant relative who might show up suddenly and raise some very serious and important questions about our behavior. So as small children with all these large creatures looming over us, we are told about this mammoth entity who will, if we are not careful, bring us to account. As I developed and grew, God was the first relationship I developed outside my family. Later I used God as a way of saying, "Now, how am I going to be good?" As I have grown older and experienced some of life's slings and arrows, I've come to feel more closely connected to Jesus. For me he is a role model for this journey in life toward eternity. More and more, I find myself turning to Jesus as a companion to help me understand what is going on. I look to him for the courage that I need to overcome my fears.

It is important to overcome our fears because our fears force us to question things. The courage we muster is the bridge between psychological answers that we think are right and the spiritual beliefs that our faith provides. We are beginning to integrate these two divergent areas. Religion, which earlier helped us cope with coming out of being primitive in molten rock, brought us to a certain point. Then science called that religion into question. Now, after focusing on science for the last few centuries, we are returning to faith and integrating it with science. We know there is more to life than being an object and we want to feel subjectively some sense of mastery in the world. Jesus is a companion with whom we can form a relationship and this relationship helps us feel we can integrate subjective parts of the world.

Doing this gives us the strength and courage to cope with fearful life experiences that will always be with us. The idea is not to find utopia—people can be miserable in utopias—but to understand how to master our fears, how to understand, experience, and integrate the fearful experiences we all have. We can learn from the example of Jesus: this man had doubts; he was afraid. Even though he may have been aware that he was in jeopardy, Jesus knew that what he was about was very important. For many of us, this awareness is the most fearful—when we consider what we need to do and begin to understand the consequences. I look to Jesus as my example who allows my faith to be a part of my sense of the world. Believing this, I can experience and understand my fears in a life-giving way.

About devils and other dark creatures

Martin C. Helldorfer

Decisions • Avoiding decisions • Moving through crisis •
Some suggestions

Brother Martin Helldorfer, F.S.C., D.Min., director of the House of Affirmation in Middletown, Connecticut, is a member of the Brothers of the Christian Schools. He served as director of novices for his community and was director of the National LaSallian Center for six years. Brother Helldorfer holds degrees in theology, chemistry, and religion and personality, and received a doctorate in counseling from Andover Newton Theological School. He is the author of The Work Trap *and* Prayer: A Guide When Troubled, *and is a frequent contributor to religious journals and periodicals.*

> *It is strange, but what do men fear most of all?*
> *A new step, a new word of their own—*
> *that's what they mostly fear.*
>
> —Dostoyevsky[1]

The focus of this paper is on the experience of being in crisis. Its message is explicit: crisis moments, while immensely uncomfortable, are still valuable. My purpose in writing is to affirm the goodness of living in such a moment, no matter how unsettling or extended it may be.

That focus is different from the one I intended. When I began to prepare my spoken presentation for the symposium, I intended to speak explicitly about the demons and devils of our dreams. However, as my preparation progressed, the focus of the presentation shifted from a consideration of the dark creatures themselves to situations that breed demons.

I have in mind a specific time and type of crisis: one that arises when we fear to make a decision or to take a step that we know we "ought" to make if we are honest with ourselves and others. I am not alluding to relatively insignificant decisions such as, "Should I buy this book?" but to decisions that involve our integrity as persons. Such times are fearful; they breed devils.

Devils need not have horns and tails. Those of us who awake time and again during the night rehearsing what is or bracing ourselves for what will be, know the experience and type of devil to which I refer.

This image of a bound person hints at the experience about which I write.[2] Notice the end of the binding rope between the man's teeth. He holds the key to his freedom or bondage within his clenched jaws. Not that he knows this or that he could loosen his grip easily. Fear makes it difficult to loosen tightened muscles.

Recently I moved into an old house and I am not yet familiar with its creaks and moans. Last night I was certain that someone had broken into the cellar; I could hear the intruder on the stairs leading up from the basement. As I lay in bed, the fear that bound me was as constricting as this man's ropes. An observer might have said: "Why don't you get up and investigate?" The advice would have fallen on deaf ears. When we are caught by fear, movement is difficult even if we know what we should do. Fortunately, no one broke into my house. The devil stealing up the stairs was of my own making.

Two weeks ago I was vacationing in Narragansett, Rhode Island as guest of the brothers who maintain a school for court-referred delinquent youths. An underground tunnel connects the two buildings on the property: the home of the retired brothers and the school.

One morning I needed to do some laundry. I went down to the cellar of one building and into the long black tunnel that led to the laundry room in the other. I could not find a switch for the tunnel lights, so I groped my way by sliding my feet along the floor. In front of me I could see a faint light coming from the laundry room some twenty or thirty yards away. Anyone watching me would have assumed by the way I walked that I expected to be injured. I recall feeling that someone crouching in the dark was about to spring at me. Eventually I found my way to the laundry. Again, there was no one hiding in the tunnel.

I relate these stories to illustrate what happens to us when we live fearfully: *our pace slows, we expect to be injured, and we find demons where there are none.*

We live in fearful times. Many persons do not feel fear, yet live fearfully. They are overly cautious persons who are on guard to avoid being hurt, and who see danger at every turn. In this paper I am not speaking to those persons. I have in mind those of us who know we are fearful. We even know the cause of our fear: the decision we are unable to make.

Decisions

The usual process in growth involves moments of crisis, times when something dies before something new is born. We can call such inevitable moments "gaps." Some of us have one never-to-be-forgotten crisis time in our lives (A). Some have three or four such moments (B). Still others feel they have never had a major crisis. For them, the new intermingles with the old in a way that smooths life's transitions (C). Still others live within the gaps most of their lives. They feel peaceful as infrequently as others feel restless (D).

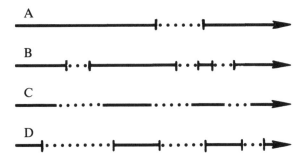

Sometimes we think something is wrong when we are in crisis. Personally, I believe crises are valuable, although uncomfortable, times. Think back over your life. When did you really grow? During peaceful times? I doubt it. When we are peaceful we tend to rest. Show me the man or woman who has avoided pain and moments of crisis and you show me someone who is undeveloped. Show me the person who has moved through crises and you show me a person of substance.

Avoiding decisions

Suppose we avoid making decisions that we know we must make if we are to remain honest with ourselves and others. Instead of moving into and through a crisis space, we become stuck. As a result, life's energies are diverted.

Usually we do not know what is happening to us. We lose interest in things, but though we feel restless, we do not know how to help ourselves. This experience, which seems so negative, is the soil from which new life grows.

To understand this possibility, I will draw on my understanding of the thoughts of three Jungian analysts: John Sanford, Fritz Kunkel, and Aldo Carotenuto.[3] First, let me explain a model which these theorists use in order to understand human experience.[4]

Imagine your psychological self as a sphere. Call the whole sphere the "self." Now place a point at the center of the sphere and call that place the "self" as well. Do not worry about the seeming contradiction of giving the same name to the whole and the center.

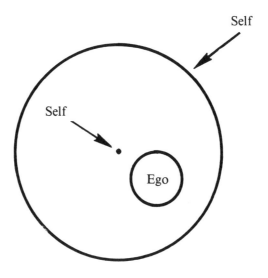

Now place a smaller sphere within the larger, and call it the "ego." The ego represents the person we are conscious of being. From this perspective, we are immensely more than we know our depth and breadth to be. In structure, we resemble icebergs. The part above the water (the ego, our conscious selves) is only the tip of a reality. No wonder theologians speak of mystery when they write of the human person as well as of God. Given this image to conceptualize our experience, consider the moment of crisis and what happens to us if we draw back from moving in the direction to which we are called.

Anxiety

Anxiety

When we are called upon to change, the ego—the person we are *aware* of being—is threatened. The threat does not come from outside us, but from the mysterious depths of our being, literally from the place we have called the "self." Using a somewhat trendy but descriptive phrase to explain what is happening, we can say that the ego is about to be dethroned. We are uncomfortable because we do not know what we fear. Anxiety arises when we are threatened by what is unseen. So anxiety is a herald of impending change and a sign of growth. Rather than search for ways to cease feeling anxious, we might seek to discover the life we are avoiding.

Lifelessness

Lifelessness

Along with anxiety, expect to feel lifeless. Usually we think of growth as a process of deciding what to do with our lives. Such conscious decision-making is important. However, there is also a way in which *growth is a process of surrendering to a development that has already taken place.* There is a way in which our lives are ahead of us. In times of major personal transition, we are two in one body: the me holding on to the person I have outgrown, and the me afraid to become the person I have already become. If we persist in clinging to the me who is outgrown, if we pull back from entering the in-between time, we feel lifeless because our vibrant life has moved ahead of us and we are holding onto a person who has died. No wonder we feel lifeless: we are living in a tomb.

Loss of creativity

Loss of creativity

As the split widens, we lose creativity. Not the unique gift of artists and great thinkers, but the creativity that all of us bring to life, as cooks, parents, ministers, salespersons, or teachers. This kind of creativity moves us out toward involvement with a liveliness and freshness that invigorates our God-given world. When we fail to surrender to new life, we lose creativity because we are content to live within the shell of a past self. Creativity flows from life, not from what is dead.

Loneliness

Loneliness

Feeling lifeless, anxious, and without creativity is, at best, uncomfortable. But refusing to surrender to needed changes also leaves us feeling lonely. There is the loneliness of knowing that no one can make the feared decision for us. There is also the loneliness of knowing that if we change, we will disappoint others, especially loved ones, which in turn breeds its own loneliness. However, those experiences are not nearly so painful as the loneliness that rises when we become alienated from our own inwardness. This loneliness makes life seem unbearable.

Depression

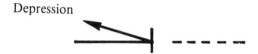

Depression follows. When loved ones die, we know how their absence changes the home. When we move ahead of ourselves and yet struggle to hold onto the past, we experience a death of sorts. The me who resists change will live with feelings of loss and heaviness up to the moment of surrender to the new life that calls us forward. We know how depressed we become when we feel betrayed. Self-betrayal is equally painful. The longer we resist the change, the deeper our depression.

Idolization and Demonization

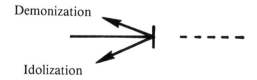

Finally, if life's energies are diverted, then the unlived life must be channeled somewhere. Often enough it is projected onto other persons. We idolize some, and demonize others. Devils are everywhere: in our dreams, on the stairs, and crouched in tunnels.

If such uncomfortable feelings and developments arise when we resist called-for changes, why would we ever pull back from life? Perhaps because the path through the in-between time is even more threatening.

Moving through crisis

The situation and dynamics explained above can be likened to the early winter experience of skating alone on an outdoor pond. Before venturing onto the ice you have to test its strength by placing one foot on the ice while keeping your other on firm ground. Remember how it felt to hear the ice snap and settle under foot? Then there is the moment when you have to decide if you are going to lift the second foot and push off. This is a moment of fear as well as trust. If we are skating alone, we may draw back in fear and decide to remain on shore. That decision might be a prudent one. But with the movement of life, we *have* to venture forth. Our problem is we feel alone in the center of the lake, and to fall through the ice is, indeed, life-threatening.

What happens if we do venture forth, notwithstanding our fears? The history of humankind is filled with stories of the consequences. None of us knows what our story will be. We can, however, expect to pay a price for venturing forth on our God-given journey. Count on the following:

Expect to feel both understood and misunderstood. Even though we fear rejection if we change, some, perhaps many, will understand and support us. However, others will misunderstand.

Growth entails moving away from being embedded in a group with a group mentality. Men and women standing out as individuals (not the same as me-centered persons) move along paths never before taken. Their journey is lonely, though not isolated.

Second, expect to feel that your decisions are dangerous. They are. Each act of liberation, however small, is accompanied by a feeling of danger because we follow unfamiliar paths.

> In other words, every forward step taken to free ourselves from whatever is holding us back is marked by fear. Everything that does not belong to the past and does not form part of our introjected experience necessarily presents itself as something threatening, because we have no ready categories by which to recognize what is happening. These categories are provided by the group, and thus every time we are afraid it may be that we are trying to do something individual. Where instead fear is absent, we are unconsciously submerged in the group and in the teachings of the past.[5]

Third, expect to feel guilty. Human life is life in relationship. We are profoundly interdependent. Life is also a process of moving from being wholly identified with others to recognizing our interdependence. That growth involves separation.

> All this is particularly obvious every time we perform an act of liberation, that is, whenever we make a qualitative leap in the sphere of emotions, ideas or work. To change . . . requires sacrifice and suffering . . . [and is] always linked to a prohibition. . . . If we succeed . . . in tolerating our sense of guilt for having broken this unwritten but no less potent law, we also succeed in grasping the creative value of our act of separation and detachment from a past that immobilizes us.[6]

These thoughts seem so ponderous. "Where is joy?" we may ask. When we live in crisis times, we do not easily find joy. My purpose in citing these dynamics is not to dwell on life's negative side, but to show that seemingly negative experiences can be valuable. Citing them is a way to say, "If you feel this way, take heart. Your experience is a sign of life. Instead of thinking that something is wrong with the way you feel, know that something is good." I want to state this opinion directly and explicitly because we live in a culture that counsels us to avoid such feelings, to forget our troubles. Those who feel strong and somewhat in control of their lives may find our culture's advice easy to follow. It is not helpful when we are feeling depressed because it leads us to mistrust our own experience and overlook the invitation to new life.

To illustrate this point, I offer the following story. A lecturer spoke of his childhood experience in pre-Nazi Germany.[7] His father held a government position at a time when the Fuehrer was coming to power. One day when the boy was playing on the steps of his home, two men approached and sat down to talk with him. They asked what the boy's father thought about the Fuehrer. His father had taught the boy to be honest at all times, so he repeated to the men some remarks his father made at table. The men thanked him and promised to return the next day.

They did return. The boy was again playing on the front steps when they arrived. They paused to thank him for being such an honest young man. Then instead of leaving, as on the previous day, they entered the house, shot his father to death in the presence of his mother, and walked calmly away. At that moment, the lecturer said, though only a boy, he *knew* the feeling of being caught between two goods: the need to be truthful as his father had taught him—and the knowledge that honesty led to his feeling he had killed his father.

Every crisis moment holds us between two goods. So we become bogged down, and change is difficult. Who wants to forfeit a known good?

To be in crisis is so uncomfortable that we often try to avoid it by surface solutions. Again, imagine that our experience can be likened to a sphere. Let point A on the surface of the sphere represent the place of crisis. We sometimes try to move out of the crisis by rebelling.

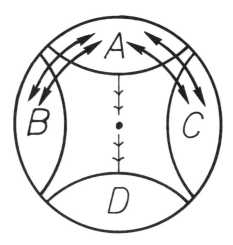

Let the rebellious solution be point B. That movement appears to be a solution, but it is not a lasting one. We look different to others, but little has changed.

Sometimes we move to the other side of the sphere to the place marked C. That solution is one of conformity. If we start to take responsibility for our lives and suffer for it, we pull back to the straight and narrow. We overvalue rules and we use willpower to shape our life decisions. This solution is no solution. We have an unlived life below the surface that is bound to trouble us as years pass.

Point D represents a place of resolution or a moment of integration. The way to that place is through the center of the sphere. That road is narrow and anyone who has been caught in crisis knows how perilous the inward journey can be. The boy who lost his father knew that journey. So does each person who faces a feared life-decision. Standing at this point in our lives, little more needs to be said. What remains is the decision to trust enough to lift the second foot from the safe place and to venture forth.

> What I enjoin on you today is not beyond your strength
> or beyond your reach.
> It is not in heaven so you need not wonder,
> "Who will go up to heaven for us to bring it down?"
> Nor is it beyond the seas, so that you need to wonder,
> "Who will cross the seas for us and bring it back?"
> No, the Word is very near to you; it is in your mouth
> and in your heart.
>
> (Deut. 30:11-14)

Some suggestions

Suggestion 1. *Risk new life.*

When we live in overly cautious and fearful ways, life's processes are greatly restricted. Violence follows.[8] Consider what happens to cultures when peoples are held in such a way that they cannot develop their gifts. "Unlived life is a destructive and irresistible force working quietly but relentlessly."[9]

Suggestion 2.
Remember the following:

(a) What we do not understand, we tend to fear. What we fear, we tend to devalue. What we devalue soon becomes a devil.

(b) When we demonize others (place our fears upon them), we have the advantage of fighting a devil outside ourselves. That path may be comfortable, but it is not the most life-giving for us or others.

(c) As uncomfortable as it is to let go of the past, it is immensely more uncomfortable to cling to it when the past has lost its life.

Suggestion 3. *Be not afraid.*

Most important, remember Jesus' counsel, "Be not afraid," and his promise to be with us always.[10]

Endnotes

1. F. Dostoyevsky, *Pensieri [Thoughts],* Eva Amendola, comp. and trans. (Rome: Bocca, 1956), p. 43. Quoted in Aldo Carotenuto's *The Vertical Labyrinth,* John Shepley, trans. (Toronto: Inner City Books, 1985), p. 62.
2. Illustration by William Steig in Wilhelm Reich's *Listen, Little Man!,* Ralph Manheim, trans. (New York: Farrar, Straus and Giroux, 1980), p. 9.
3. See *Fritz Kunkel: Selected Writings,* edited and with Introduction and Commentary by John A. Sanford (New York: Paulist Press, 1984), and Carotenuto, *The Vertical Labyrinth.* Also "Individuation," John Sanford, taped lectures, Paulist Press, 1984.
4. The model I have used is developed in John Sanford's introduction to Fritz Kunkel's *Selected Writings.*
5. Carotenuto, p. 19.
6. Ibid., p. 32.
7. Personal story told by 1983 lecturer at the Jung Institute in Zurich. I do not remember his name.
8. Eugene Mihaesco, *New York Times Book Review,* December, 1985.
9. Carl Jung, *Selected Writings,* Jolande Jacobe, ed. (New York: Harper Torchback, 1960), p. 107.
10. See Matthew 28:10, 20.

When all children are created equal: The fear of telling

Audrey E. Campbell

The experience • The picture •
Preconditions for sexual abuse •
The re-experience of telling •
The curtain

Audrey E. Campbell, Ph.D., a psychotherapist at the House of Affirmation in Whitinsville, Massachusetts, has graduate degrees in theology from St. John's University, New York and in applied spirituality from the University of San Francisco. She received her master's and doctoral degrees in clinical psychology from the Psychological Studies Institute in Palo Alto, California. Dr. Campbell, a psychotherapist, art therapist, and spiritual director, has conducted numerous workshops and retreats on issues of psychological and spiritual health and growth. She is a member of several professional organizations including the American Psychological Association and the American Art Therapy Association.

The experience

The view

Looking in this window
      more like the door to her soul
We see the building of a most appalling scenario.
She is a girl
     young
       sad
         slow moving
As if thinking thoughts far too heavy laden.
Mother comes and goes . . .
      surely mother knows.

She busies herself far busier than her chores demand.
The kitchen sparkles and the dishes shine.
She polishes and shines.
She makes the children's lunches,
    she makes her own.
She's staving off the night
Hoping that the beer will overcome
    before the darkness.
She stirs the children
    and they laugh and run about a bit
But they are far too tired to hold out for long
    Besides . . .
The darkness has come
    and he sits and waits.
Mother comes and goes . . .
    to bed.
The terror is complete.

The victim

Who will help me through this night? Alone, I'm all alone. The sky lights up the room. I wish it were the morning sun, but it's the moon. I don't want to be touched. Do not touch! Do not touch! Do not . . . no, no, I have to get prepared. It's not so bad, it will be over soon. I know he loves me. I don't know why he wants to do that all the time anyway. It's awful, it's disgusting, it hurts. Don't scream. Here he comes. Be quiet or mother will know. Be quiet or the children will see. Be quiet or I'll wake God and then God will know.

The view

Looking in this window
            more like the door to his soul
We see the building of a most appalling scenario.
He is a boy
            growing tall and strong in body
            fragile and uncertain in mind
He sits on crumpled clothes
            on a crumpled bed
Staring through walls
            through space
            through things
His mind unfocused
            because it won't
His decision not made
            because he can't
He moves to his feet.
The beautiful new sweater
From his mother's favorite brother
            he grabs
And runs through the door
            to his summer vacation.

The victim

I can't tell Mom, she has enough to worry about. Dad will think
I'm queer. Uncle must think so, Father must have thought so, those
boys at school must have seen it. Maybe Uncle won't hurt me this
time. He said he's the only one who really loves me.

The picture

Such agonizing pictures often unfold slowly, sometimes after
years of forgetting, repressing, and avoiding. The picture unfolds
in dreams, in art, in moments of fantasy or through the process of
therapy. The pain emerges in living, relating, withdrawing, and
remembering. The pain sometimes emerges in repetition.

Some professional estimates suggest that as much as 50% of child sexual abuse goes unreported. According to varying statistics, from 8% to 22% of all American children have been victims of child sexual abuse. The National Organization of Rape Crises Intervention Facilities speaks of one in four girls and one in six boys being victimized by sexual abuse before the age of eighteen. Child sexual abuse crosses the lines of race, religion, economic status. However, it cannot be denied that poverty increases the vulnerability of the child to sexual abuse and substantially raises the probability. Being a foster child, a stepchild, and in some cases, an adopted child increases the child's chances of falling victim. Being the child of a dysfunctional or absent mother increases the child's chances of falling victim. Some 97% of reported child abuse is carried out by men—mostly against girls—but evidence indicates that massive numbers of cases of abused boys go unreported to authorities. It seems to be true that abusive adults were abused children and suffer from seriously faulty development of their own inner selves.

Definitions

A *Los Angeles Times* survey of 2,627 randomly chosen adults defined child sexual abuse as attempted or completed sexual intercourse, oral copulation or sodomy, fondling, touching, taking nude photographs, and exhibitionism.

Those polled broadened that definition to include such acts as making indecent suggestions to a child and said that even attempted sexual acts must count as abuse.

Physical abuse when accompanied by sexual overtones should be included, as when a father strips and beats his fourteen-year-old daughter or son.

A thin line can be drawn to include children subjected to seductiveness of overt or subtle psychological means by parent or relative or teacher or clergy or neighbor.

In his study of child sexual abuse, David Finklehorr proposes four preconditions and develops a theory moving toward more clarity and understanding of the phenomena.[1]

Preconditions for sexual abuse

	Level of explanation	
	Individual	Social/Cultural
Precondition I: Factors related to motivation to sexually abuse someone		
Emotional congruence	Arrested emotional development Need to feel powerful and controlling Re-enactment of childhood trauma to undo the hurt Narcissistic identification with self as a young child	Masculine requirement to be dominant and powerful in sexual relationships
Sexual arousal	Childhood sexual experience that was traumatic or strongly conditioning Modeling of sexual interest in children by someone else Misattribution of arousal cues Biologic abnormality	Child pornography Erotic portrayal of children in advertising Male tendency to sexualize all emotional needs
Blockage	Oedipal conflict Castration anxiety Fear of adult females Traumatic sexual experience with adult Inadequate social skills Marital problems	Repressive norms about masturbation and extra-marital sex

	Individual	Social
Precondition II: Factors predisposing to overcoming internal inhibitors	Alcohol Psychosis Impulse disorder Senility Failure of incest inhibition mechanism in family dynamics	Social tolerance of sexual interest in children Weak criminal sanctions against offenders Ideology of patriarchal prerogatives for fathers Social toleration for deviance committed while intoxicated Child pornography Male inability to identify with needs of children
Precondition III: Factors predisposing to overcoming external inhibitors	Mother who is absent or ill Mother who is not close to or protective of child Mother who is dominated or abused by father Social isolation of family Unusual opportunities to be alone with child Lack of supervision of child Unusual sleeping or rooming conditions	Lack of social supports for mother Barriers to women's equality Erosion of social networks Ideology of family sanctity
Precondition IV: Factors predisposing to overcoming child's resistance	Child who is emotionally insecure or deprived Child who lacks knowledge about sexual abuse Situation of unusual trust between child and offender Coercion	Unavailability of sex education for children Social powerlessness of children

The re-experience of telling

The victim

"Last night I dreamed. . . ."
"I saw this TV show and I remembered. . . ."
"An image keeps coming to mind. . . ."
"Who could believe this. . . ?"
"I can't sleep in the dark. . . ."
"He didn't mean it. . . ."
"They didn't care for me. . . ."
"Will you still love me after I tell you this . . . ?"

No words can express the agony and shame that precede, accompany, and follow telling.

In the telling there is healing
                darkness
                        years of tears
                                killing rage

There is a sarcastic flippancy that accompanies self-devaluation. There is an inner self that is fragmented. Inner peace is a stranger; loveableness is unknown; suspicion reigns; trust is laughable; touch is fearful; relationships falter; sexual activity is unexplained and sometimes compulsive.

And the self, the wounded inner self, longs for healing.

The healing

In the empathy that reaches out from one self to another
In the listening, regarding, caring, believing, *believing*
In the mutual rage, even outrage
In the gentle perseverance
In the sitting Zen of therapeutic hours
You can tell. You have *already* survived.
And you *can* survive the telling.

The curtain

When all children are created equal in our eyes: we will see their pain and rescue them from abuse; we will run swiftly to save them; we will name games and call things by their right names; and run to save the children.

When all children are created equal in our society: we will end the violent and sexual exploitation of our children in ads and magazines, in pornography and prostitution, in jokes and innuendos, in our pedagogies of child-rearing, in our hospitals and detention systems, in our Congress and political systems.

When all children are created equal in our churches: we will end the phenomenon of hidden clerical sexual abuse of our children; we will explore the phenomenon of sexual exploitation of our youth in seminaries and novitiates; we will balance the sexism that our religious traditions have taken for granted.

When all children are created equal in our attitudes: we will consider children as endowed with inalienable rights to the sanctity and integrity of their own minds and bodies; we will *ask before we touch* them; we will touch them only nonsexually and appropriately; we will never permit them to be used to satisfy another person's sexual desires, and when they say that something is abusive we will *believe* them.

When all children are created equal in our hearts we will free the bondaged child within by surviving and telling and *surviving the telling*.

Endnote

1. David Finklehorr, *Child Sexual Abuse: New Theory and Research* (New York: The Free Press [Macmillan], 1984), pp. 56-57. Chapter 5, "Four Preconditions: A Model," pp. 53-68, gives an explanation of the complexities noted in the Table, as well as clinical treatment implications.

Fear of failure

Joseph L. Hart

Obstacles to self-direction • Anxiety that restricts us •
Genesis of the fear of failure • Attitudinal changes •
Importance of trust

Reverend Joseph L. Hart, S.S.E., Ph.D., is a psychotherapist at the House of Affirmation in Whitinsville, Massachusetts. A member of the Society of St. Edmund, Father Hart received his undergraduate degree from St. Michael's College, Burlington, Vermont, his doctorate from the Catholic University of America, and a certificate in psychotherapy from the Alfred Adler Institute in Chicago, Illinois. Father Hart has served as the director of the Whitinsville and Middletown centers, and was a consultant to Heronbrook House, the House of Affirmation affiliate in England, when it opened. Father Hart is a member of the American Society of Group Psychotherapy and Psychodrama, and the North American Society of Adlerian Psychology.

If a man has a talent and cannot use it, he has failed.
—Thomas Wolfe

Carl Jung was reportedly one day seated on a train departing from the Zurich Bahnhof. The conductor benignly observed the eighty-four-year-old master of analytic psychology going through his briefcase in a vain search for his ticket. Jung was well-known to the Swiss conductor, so the genial official reassured his famous passenger.

"Herr Doctor will find his ticket after the journey, and mail it to the railroad office."

Jung immediately sat up, and replied with spirit: "All well and good, my friend, but the problem is not the missing ticket. The problem is, where am I going?"[1]

"Where am I going?" is a question we ask ourselves often in life. We give different responses to it at different periods of our lives but it is an important question because it helps us to form our goals: what it is we want to achieve and accomplish; what it is we want to do and *be*. "Where am I going?" is answered by us sometimes implicitly and sometimes explicitly; sometimes completely and at other times incompletely; sometimes in a helpful way and sometimes in a harmful way; but it is a question that is constantly present: "Where am I going?"

Obstacles to self-direction

There are many hindrances to reaching the goals we have set for ourselves; hindrances to what we want to do with our lives and what we want to be. They come from things we can do nothing about as well as situations over which we have control. Examples of the former are the tone deaf youngster who would love to be a concert pianist or the youth with poor coordination who looks forward to playing big league baseball. Then there are things that we could do but we have not made them important goals in our life. They are our "wishes" or "shoulds"; things we would "like" to do but not enough to really do them! "I should lose weight" is different from "I want to diet" or "I shouldn't eat so much candy (or smoke, or nap so often)" is quite different from saying a direct no to these habits. We have good intentions without action; what an old professor of mine used to call being "full of should." The problem lies in the decision-making process.

So we encounter obstacles to reaching our goals that come from things we can do nothing about and from things that we can do something about, even if, at times, we do not care to. In fact, there are many hindrances that help keep us from reaching our goals, from going in the direction we want to, including our own emotions and feelings. For example, there is the feeling of depression that saps our energy so we are not able to push ourselves toward our goal. There is the feeling of anxiety that, at times, can be so strong it keeps us from making meaningful contacts with other people. If our anxiety is very intense we may even avoid crowds of strangers.

In severe cases this anxiety can result in panic and we turn all our energy toward one goal, escape. There is also a flight from the internal dangers not clearly seen by the individual and when the person cannot escape, a temporary disintegration of the personality can result.[2]

The feeling that is going to receive our attention in this chapter is the fear of failure, of not succeeding in doing something before one even starts. This fear can be a major hindrance in reaching our goals and objectives.

Here I would like to make a distinction between fear and anxiety and the way we use these words. Fear is a threat to the periphery of our existence whereas anxiety strikes at the center core of our self-esteem and our sense of value as a self. Fear can be objectified; we can stand outside it and look at it. Fear can be healthy: it is a useful and rational kind of fright elicited by external dangers.[3] Anxiety, in a greater or lesser degree, overwhelms our awareness of existence, blocks out the sense of time, dulls our memory of the past, and erases the future. Rollo May gives the following example:

> The anxiety a person feels when someone he respects passes him on the street without speaking is not as intense as the fear he experiences when the dentist seizes the drill to attack a sensitive tooth. But the gnawing threat of the slight on the street may hound him all day long and torment his dreams at night, whereas the feeling of fear, though it was quantitatively greater, is gone forever as soon as he steps out of the dentist's chair.[4]

So fear and anxiety are not the same; they are distinct reactions as May's example illustrates. However, at times we use the word *fear* to name both reactions. The feeling that may come when we have to climb a ladder to a dangerous position is a reaction of fear; we perceive an objective and realistic danger. But when we use the word *fear* in "fear of failure" we mean an emotional reaction that we might have to being ridiculed or making a fool of ourselves, that we will not succeed in a given situation. This is the anxiety that goes right to the core of our identity, that attacks our self-concept. Such a fear is the apprehension of public speaking, especially before a group that we feel will be critical of us.

Anxiety that restricts us

The fear of failure is one of the most limiting of all the anxieties. It keeps us from trying: we do not want to risk the embarrassment of failure. It keeps us from entering the arena of life and being involved, of doing things, of being engaged with others and taking risks. It gives us excuses for not making these efforts and so it limits our lives. It is personally very constrictive and it takes away our freedom. It is the most neuroticizing of all fears.

Many examples can be mentioned in addition to speaking or performing before a group where the fear of failure is often present because the fearful individuals think the group will ridicule them or find fault with their performance. There is also the person who has good research material for writing and publishing an article, or one who feels strongly about a particular topic, but fears that once the ideas are down on paper they are carved in granite for all to see and criticize. The article is never written because of the fear that significant people will find fault with some positions taken in the article. There is also apprehension about changing our opinion on an important topic, or taking a new position, because people frequently ask us to explain or justify the change. Rather than risk failure, we say nothing. We choose not to make ourselves vulnerable.

Another fear of failure affects us in social relationships and in making friends. We fear that we will not know what to say or how to converse; that we might make a mistake; that we will be seen as socially inept. Because this fear of failure in social situations keeps us from building relationships it promotes loneliness, which in turn reinforces the fear of failure and thus creates a vicious circle.

Ordinary stage fright is a common reaction experienced by many of us, if not all! It consists of anticipatory fears before stressful events like examinations, or public performances and public speaking, or social gatherings, or important occasions like going on a date. These fears are more or less normal reactions.

Stage fright can help the actor or actress to give a better performance or the speaker to deliver a better speech. It prods the performers to be at their best and to proceed with the function despite the apprehensive feeling of stage fright.

The fear of failure to which we refer is more intense than normal stage fright. It is an anxiety that can cripple because it is so closely related to our self-esteem, to our feelings of our own value, dignity, and worth. It is a foreboding fear that we will make mistakes and look ridiculous.

Subjective aspect

It is important to note the following points:

1. The presumption that we will fail, or nearly fail, is usually anticipatory. The apprehension is so great that physiological changes occur in the body: our voice trembles, we "choke up" or perspire excessively, we have sweaty palms and wobbly knees. In the fear of failure these signs occur because we anticipate a problem in our performance before we begin and so we never start. If we should begin and the fear continues, then the physiological changes interfere with our performance.

2. The most important aspect of this fear is its subjectivity. We are not talking about the rational fear of a realistic failure. If I have never flown an airplane and I am in a small one when the pilot has a heart attack, then my fear of being unable to land the plane safely is realistic. But the fear that I will not perform adequately when under public scrutiny is subjective, coming from an inner judgment that I make about myself and those observing my activity. For example, a child may be able to work out a math problem correctly at home but fears failing if she does it at the classroom chalkboard. She feels the observers will be harsh in their judgments. Or think of the man who prepares a speech but fears audience ridicule if he should make a mistake and so avoids delivering the talk. Again, a woman may play beautiful music in the privacy of her own home, but refuse to perform before a group. The fear of failure, subjective as it is, restricts public activity.

According to Karen Horney, the subjective element in the fear of failure is very significant. She saw this anxiety as presumed ridicule and/or a loss of esteem in one's own eyes.[5] For example, all the members of the graduating class may be required to take achievement tests. One student who majored in ancient history may have very high expectations for himself and want the best mark obtainable, but fears beforehand that he will not succeed. Then there is his classmate who majored in auto body repair and has no expectations for herself in the history section of the exam. She does not have the fear of failure, while the history major may experience himself as a failure if he gets a B instead of an A +.

The subjective element is present when we interpret an event according to our inner or private logic while it may well be interpreted differently by others. This element of subjectivity was well illustrated by Jean Rhys in her novel, *Good Morning, Midnight:*

> Walking in the night with the dark houses over you, like monsters.
>
> If you have money and friends, houses are just houses with steps and a front door—friendly houses when a door opens and some-one meets you, smiling.
>
> If you are quite secure and your roots are well struck in, they know.
>
> They stand back respectfully, waiting for the poor devil without any friends and without any money. Then they step forward, the waiting houses, to frown and crush.
>
> No hospitable doors, no lit windows, just frowning darkness.
>
> Frowning and leering and sneering, the houses, one after another.
>
> Tall cubes of darkness, with two lighted eyes at the top to sneer.
>
> And they know who to frown at. They know as well as the police-man on the corner, and don't you worry.[6]

I don't know if you have experienced anything like that, but I know I have, especially lost in a strange city at night! The houses *seem* overpowering—they take on unpleasant personalities in my subjective and insecure feelings.

This fear of failure is also based on what we think and feel about mistakes. The influence of our culture on this issue must be carefully considered. Our society is very achievement oriented: success gathers respect, failure loses esteem, and mistakes are too often seen as failures. Mistakes are unavoidable; they are part of human living. Mistakes *can* be learning experiences that help us find more effective ways of dealing with problems. Yet too often youngsters begin to question their self-esteem because of the criticism made of their mistakes. Too often children are compared in a harmful way to someone else—another student, an older sibling—and they lose that important feeling of personal security.

Much too often when youngsters begin school their unbridled and healthy curiosity is dashed against the rocks by significant people, teachers, parents, older siblings. When children's mistakes are ridiculed or criticized they may feel they are *personally* being ridiculed or criticized, and their self-esteem lessens. They often get large doses of discouragement following an error when it is encouragement they need. Youngsters need to feel they are o.k. even when they make mistakes, that mistakes are normal, and they can learn from them.

Encouragement, praise, and affirmation are too often given only to the successful, who do not need them. Less successful children are more in need of encouragement, praise, and affirmation but usually do not receive them. Many of us still carry scars from inappropriate treatment we received as youngsters, and so we are tainted with the fear of failure because we easily anticipate ridicule that we see as personal disgrace.

View of principle issues

We have discussed the fear of failure as inhibiting our freedom to perform; we have noted that it is mostly anticipatory, although it can operate when the task is in process.

The fear of failure is subjective and so it depends upon our opinion of the situation and of ourselves. This fear will, of course, vary from person to person but we know we humans are similar enough to each other to recognize many situations that are common pitfalls: performing in public, taking exams, learning new skills, social interactions, assuming new jobs and responsibilities, and so on.

We must also be aware that the fear of failure needs to be understood in an interpersonal context. The fearful person is afraid of losing value in the estimation of others.[7]

Contributions from research

Social psychologists have done research on the fear of failure, and have found other reasons for its damaging influence.

For instance, by doing poorly in an achievement situation, we are faced with the possibility of self-devaluation.[8] This occurs when we are afraid of not performing as superbly as our exacting "shoulds" demand, and therefore we fear our pride will be hurt.[9] Some men and women have set extremely high standards of behavior for themselves and are afraid they cannot reach their own expectations. Finally, there are people who fear they will be punished or lose an anticipated reward by failing. All three causes: (1) anticipating ridicule from others with consequent loss of self-esteem; (2) self-devaluation in one's own eyes; and (3) punishment, usually by losing an award, may operate simultaneously, but we usually feel a "watcher" or "watchers" are present, evaluating our performance, and criticizing. That is why the fear of failure must be understood in an interpersonal context—our great concern with what others think of our performance constricts us. It is interesting to see how we give others so much power over us.

Men and women who fear failure seem more inclined to anticipate failure than do success-oriented persons. I knew a woman who was a successful teacher in her classroom but extremely fearful of making presentations in front of other groups. She was determined to avoid those faculty or parent meetings where she might have to give a report. Rather than talk before them she avoided the task through all kinds of excuses and manipulations. She exaggerated her possible failure beforehand and so subconsciously gave herself the permission to avoid the risky events. The few times she had to speak she did so adequately. On these occasions she distorted the objective probabilities of failure downward, and so she was able to get through the task keeping her fear of failure intact.

Genesis of the fear of failure

How do people develop fears of failure so they lessen their achievement goals and lower their level of aspiration by avoiding selected situations? We have seen one contributing factor, the emphasis of a mistake-centered educational system in which the children develop a poor self-image, at least in some areas. But other youngsters may go through the same school system, have the same teachers, be in the same classrooms, and not develop such marked fears of failure. The home environment often promotes poor self-esteem by undue criticism and fault finding, comparisons with other siblings, and by promoting feelings of nonbelonging with resultant feelings of insecurity. If we add this type of home environment to a poor school situation we can see how children gallop toward a faulty self-image that supports the fear of failure.

But suppose one sibling from a family goes to the same school and has the same teachers as the other sibling and is treated similarly by significant members of the family, yet does not develop these pronounced fears? The fact is that two children from the same family do not have the same environment; each new birth changes the home situation and the family dynamics. Children who develop fears of failure may have an undue sensitivity to the real or imagined opinions of others about themselves. They may find their significance in the eyes of important people (parents or teachers) by not failing. They may believe they are more acceptable to the significant people in their lives by not failing and this belief becomes so important to them that possible achievements are less important than avoiding risks of real failure. Another hypothesis suggests that children may be pushed beyond their capabilities and so experience an unusual number of failures. "With a background of failure experiences one would suppose that such people would generally have a lower self-estimate than the average person."[10]

These anxieties may also arise from children who were overprotected in their youth and enjoyed the pampered lifestyle of royalty. They are the really "spoiled" youngsters with whom we come in contact. When these spoiled children become adults they do not realize their own strengths and abilities because they did not have opportunities to exercise them when they were younger. As children they were discouraged from taking risks. Their fear of failure is based on self-doubt with the consequent avoidance of risks. The constricting part, again, is that they have to lower their achievement goals in their own lives—they cannot aspire too high; it is too risky.

As we can see, the roots of this anxiety can be many and varied, and more than one variable may operate at the same time. I would like to mention one more factor because it contributes so much to this anxiety, not only in youngsters but also in adults, including religious and clergy: perfectionism.

While it may seem highly desirable to try to be as good and right as possible, perfectionism has been called a "faulty social value." Perfectionism can serve personal superiority or self-elevation, helping us to feel or think we are better than others.[11] It is also a faulty social value when we create high standards for ourselves without recognizing that they are ideals, and as such usually not attainable. (If they are, we tend to make new ones or to push the old ones higher.) It is important to be motivated by high ideals, but it is equally important to recognize that reality often falls short of the ideals. The fear of failure begins to operate when we believe that our high standards must be reached at all times or *we* are failures. It is easy to see how a series of failures would develop fears of failing that would keep us from acting. There would be no movement, no striving for achievement, because of our fear of failure. Nothing happens except that the high ideals remain intact in our fantasy, unchallenged.

Attitudinal changes

I hope that an understanding of this neuroticizing anxiety will be the first step to bringing it under control. Fear of failure is a behavior in which we engage, a feeling we create out of the perception that others will adversely judge our performance and so we will suffer a loss of value, of personal esteem, of acceptance. It is more a behavior than a personality type or trait. We are afraid of ridicule by others. We fear that lack of success will be harmful to our self-image and perhaps bring upon us punishment or at least the withholding of rewards. Because this interpersonal aspect is usually present we give others control over us. This fear of failure is also subjective so that a situation that is fearful for one person may not be fearful for another. Its effect is based on perfectionism or an exaggerated fear of making mistakes. It is influenced by messages we learned in childhood from significant people telling us that we are incompetent, mistake-prone, failures! And how can we as failures hope to succeed?

So, the question of what to do begins with an understanding of what this anxiety is, and how we learn it. This mistaken learning can be discarded and replaced by new learning. (I am aware that Jung, whom I mentioned in the opening of this talk, noted that the most difficult actions are usually simple to state.)

For example, we have seen how a fear of failure precludes risks. But if we do not risk we do not grow. Abraham Maslow pointed out how frequently we experience the tension between the known, the old, the comfortable, the secure on the one hand, and the risk involved in trying something new, unknown, and insecure on the other.[12] A toddler will not learn to walk without the risk of standing up, of getting one foot off the ground and moving it in front of the other, and of keeping balance. Only when risks are taken can growth take place. Maslow also pointed out how risks will readily be taken only when a safety factor is present. Toddlers learning to walk have the safety factor of one set of adult hands extended to meet them while another pair supports them in their first few faltering steps. When the safety factor is present the risk is readily taken, the pleasure of learning follows, and real growth takes place.

Importance of trust

A colleague of mine, Dr. Ed Franasiak, wrote about the importance of trust for youngsters during their formative years. He pointed out that trust is basic to all relationships and to human development; it provides a needed safety factor. Following Eric Erickson, Franasiak referred to trust as the assumption that someone is there, that original optimism without which we cannot live.

Franasiak relates a story that illustrates how trust, as a safety factor, encourages risk:

> Once upon a time there were a father and a son. The building in which they lived was old and in disrepair. One evening after they went to bed a great fire broke out. The father ran out of the building thinking his son was safe, only to find that the son had climbed to the roof and was trapped. "Jump!" he called to his son. "I can't, I can't," cried the child. "Jump!" begged the father. "I'm afraid, I can't," was the answer. The smoke thickened; the flames billowed. Again the father screamed, "Jump, son, jump. I'll catch you!" "No," screamed the child. "I'm afraid; I cannot see you." "But I can see you," cried the father. "Jump, now!" And the son jumped. The father caught him; the child was saved. [13]

This story illustrates how trust is a necessary element in risk-taking, enabling us to act courageously despite our fear.

We meet hundreds of tension-producing situations throughout life. It is a challenge for a child to meet a new playmate, to learn a new game, to go to school for the first time. Challenges, risks, fears, growth, fun—all were involved in learning to swim or to ride a bicycle. As we get older other tensions between the known and comfortable and the unknown and risky are present: making new friends; going to high school or college; dating; moving; changing jobs; making career and vocation choices; beginning work opportunities within a particular vocation; marrying; raising children. I am sure you can name other tensions that are part of any life, and that increase the more intensely the person lives.

Children are helped to take risks despite the possibility, even the likelihood, of failing when the parents help them feel secure by promoting a feeling of belonging, by treating them as "good," even when they make mistakes, and by encouraging growth through their own attitudes. Then children are willing to risk because the hope of success is stronger than the fear of failure.

For adults, safety factors are also necessary. Good friends and loyal family members can provide this personal support. Community members and clerical colleagues can also be good and loyal friends who help minimize the fear of failure and maximize the hope of success by their noncritical attitude of personal acceptance.

Talking things over with people who are important to us helps us to objectify the anxiety, to bring it out of ourselves into the light, and to examine it in conversation with others. Planning other options in case one choice does not work out is another safety factor that lessens our fear of failure and makes risk-taking more palatable with consequent personal growth.

Encouraging others to express their tensions and fear of failure helps them deal with this fear. We are thus part of their support system. We need to let those close to us know that their mistakes do not decrease their personal value to us. Maintaining our acceptance of them lessens their fear of ridicule by others.

Let me emphasize this suggestion by summarizing it. A mature attitude toward this anxiety, both for ourselves and for others, values growth, so the risk is worth taking despite the fear of failure.

We can be slaves to the reactions, real or presumed, of others toward us; if we minimize that attitude, then the fear of failure lessens because we are not so concerned about "losing face." We discussed this interpersonal element earlier. To be free of the opinions of others is a difficult goal indeed, but one worth having and working toward, however imperfectly.

A realistic attitude recognizes that mistakes are unavoidable and part of life; everybody makes them, even presidents and popes. Mistakes do not decrease the value of the person, although many of us make this subjective mistake, thinking that an error reflects on our personal worth.

It would help to look at our Lord's attitude toward mistakes. For example, others would stone the woman taken in adultery; he accepted her. Christ gave us the parable of the prodigal son to illustrate the mercy and love of his Father and himself. In the parable the human father is as accepting of his sons, despite their mistakes, as a father could possibly be. And recall Christ's instruction to Peter who generously suggested he forgive mistake-makers seven times: the Lord said to forgive them seventy times seven times!

Often it is easier for us to be understanding and forgiving toward others when they make mistakes than it is to be tolerant toward ourselves; we find it difficult to be a Christian toward ourselves.

Review of suggestions

Let us summarize the suggestions of what to do about fear of failure. We have seen that it is helpful to have a good personal support group, to talk about this anxiety with others, to have alternatives ready if one plan does not work, to value growth despite the risks involved, and to have a reasonable attitude toward mistakes. The most important suggestion concerns the streak of perfectionism that is so strong in many of us, perhaps all of us. We often set high standards for ourselves that are practically unreachable so we build in the fear of failure from the beginning.

Religious and clergy especially seem to have a tendency to create high ideals without realizing that they are goals for which to aim, but not necessarily achieve. Reality is frequently less than the ideal would have it. But this condition is human.

We can whittle away at our attitude of perfectionism so that we do not feel that we must handle every situation perfectly or otherwise we are failures. We do not have to be a faultless speaker, an errorless author; we do not have to be the social success of every conversation and social gathering, nor do we have to be the best at everything we do. We need only to be human, to be our selves. But this attitude takes courage. Paradoxically, we can lessen the fear of failure syndrome by our courage to be imperfect.

Endnotes

1. *Voices* 15 (Fall 1979): 44.
2. Freida Fromm-Reichmann, "Psychiatric Aspects of Anxiety," *Identity and Anxiety,* Maurice Stern et al., eds. (New York: Free Press, 1960), p. 130.
3. Ibid.
4. Rollo May, "Contributions of Existential Psychotherapy," *Creative Developments in Psychotherapy,* Alvin R. Mahrer and Leonard Pearson, eds. (Cleveland: Case Western Reserve University, 1971), p. 117.
5. Karen Horney, *Neurosis and Human Growth* (New York: W. W. Norton, 1950), p. 100.
6. Jean Rhys, *Good Morning, Midnight.* Quoted in *The New York Times Book Review,* Sept. 18, 1985, p. 43.
7. Robert C. Birney et al., eds., *Fear of Failure* (New York: Van Nostrand-Reinhold, 1969), p. 4.
8. Ibid., p. 225.
9. Horney, *Neurosis and Human Growth,* p. 101.
10. Birney, *Fear of Failure,* p. 20.
11. Rudolph Dreikurs, *Psychodynamics, Psychotherapy, and Counseling* (Chicago: Alfred Adler Institute, 1967), pp. 115-120.
12. A. H. Maslow, "A Theory of Human Motivation," *Readings in the Psychology of Adjustment,* Leon Gorlow and Walter Katlovsky, eds. (New York: McGraw-Hill, 1959), pp. 206-214.
13. E. J. Franasiak, "Betrayed: The anger of growing up," *Anger: Issues of Emotional Living in an Age of Stress for Clergy and Religious,* Brendan P. Riordan, ed. (Whitinsville, Mass.: Affirmation Books, 1985), pp. 36-37.

Fear and the critic

David E. Doiron

Fear as anticipation •
Mechanisms to deal with fear •
Learning about the critic • Dealing with our critic

Reverend David E. Doiron, D.Min., a psychotherapist at the House of Affirmation in Hopedale, Massachusetts, is a priest of the diocese of Worcester, Massachusetts. He pursued his graduate education at the University of Louvain, Belgium, and Assumption College, Worcester, Massachusetts, and received a doctorate in ministry from Andover Newton Theological School. Before joining the staff of the House of Affirmation, Father Doiron was director of the Wachusett satellite of the Worcester Pastoral Counseling Center, and chief psychological evaluator and tribunal judge for the Diocese of Worcester Marriage Tribunal. Father Doiron is a member of the American Association of Pastoral Counselors and the American Association of Marriage and Family Counselors.

There are many occasions for fear. A woman being chased down a dark street at night, a student taking a driving test or a family waiting for a severe hurricane to strike—all these people experience fear.

Theorists note that fear and anger are two basic emotions necessary and useful in emergencies.[1] They are part of a biological response mechanism that helps keep us alive.

In higher animals such as humans, pain and pleasure serve as a regulating mechanism to insure survival and security. Pain and pleasure not only indicate what is good or bad, but they also help us to take appropriate action. What is painful is a threat to survival and must be avoided; what is pleasurable brings survival and must be sought. In the primitive stages of human cultural development, this emotion greatly facilitated survival.

But pain is not fear. Pain will help me to know whether I like eating bear meat, but it will not help me if I am being eaten by the bear. Pain has only limited escape value. I need some way to see the bear approaching, to anticipate it. With the senses of smell, hearing, and vision, my distance receptors, I can hope to locate the bear before the bear finds me. Distance receptors make anticipation possible and anticipation is an important instrument in our struggle for survival.

Fear as anticipation

Fear is the anticipation of a painful experience. It is what I feel when I see the bear coming toward me. Fear is part of a larger emotional complex mobilizing me for action.

Anxiety is different from fear, usually more vague, with no specific source. It is more unconsciously oriented. Our imagination and reasoning powers facilitate anxiety, and our capacity for symbol formation can precipitate it. We do not have to see the real thing to be anxious. Often something that we associate with a danger can trigger the memory of an event or person which brings about anxiety. Seeing bear tracks in the snow might evoke a scary memory of a past event and arouse my anxiety in the present.

However, signs are not always true predictors; they may introduce distortions because of my individual past history. Yet, this capacity for symbolization allows me to anticipate and gives me strength and stability beyond my weight, size, and normal power. I can run from the bear or prepare to face it; I can change the reality itself. In this way I become co-author with nature in an active way.

Today most of our fears do not come from anticipation of a real danger in our environment but rather by a change in our sense of self. Anything that questions our confidence threatens our safety. Whatever weakens our sense of strength, or attacks our pride and self-esteem makes us feel more helpless and vulnerable. Any threat to our competitive and survival powers generates fear. Our need for approval and acceptance can also be a focus for fear.

One of the earliest lessons babies learn is that weakness does not mean destruction. The first method of survival is not fight or flight, but clutch and cling.

Infants often have a delusional sense of power: usually when they scream or cry they are fed. When children begin to differentiate or separate from their mother, they begin to experience their own helplessness. At the same time, however, they realize that their parents are powerful and can supply their needs if the parents so desire. The question is, "Are they willing?" The child then learns that the parents' willingness to supply their child's needs is related to their feelings about the child. So the child thinks, "As long as they love me, cherish me, and value me, they will take care of me. Even if I'm weak, I can be strong if my helplessness generates protective feelings in my powerful parents." Therefore, the first lesson we learn is, "I am safe if I am loved." Consequently the most powerful fear is not to be weak, but to be unloved. All that is needed to provoke separation fear is the most fleeting, imagined, accidental or insignificant incident.

When another person criticizes me, even wrongly, I feel anxious because I need to be approved, not to be right. The judgment of the group or its representative threatens my survival, not the facts.

Consequently, the experience of disapproval or the simple absence of positive signs can trigger fear and anxiety in me.

Another source of everyday fear is the awareness of our inevitable vulnerability: death. We do not want to believe it. But the price we pay for our denial is that we see death everywhere. We are anxious not because of the insecurity of our role in life, but because of its limitation: it will end.

Mechanisms to deal with fear

Given the fact that the world is always changing, we seem condemned to constant fear and anxiety. Fortunately, we have mechanisms for avoiding or dissipating fear and anxiety. For instance, fear is often most troublesome when it appears irrational and illegitimate. So we displace the fear onto something we can control, such as a cause, even an incorrect one. Children may displace their fear of parents onto animals, thereby not only rationalizing the fear but also controlling and limiting it.

Another way to dissipate fear is through somatization when we convert the fear into physical symptoms. If we are afraid to speak in front of a group, we may feel sick to our stomach.

These mechanisms do not always work well, but they make our fear more tolerable as they control its level.

Sometimes we soften the threat by directly confronting its underlying reason. I say to myself, "I am fearful because I am weak and vulnerable. I will prove I am superior to others by spending money and show my power and care for myself." Or I seek reassurances from friends. Sex can also be used to prove my self-worth and lovableness.

One of the most prevalent ways of relieving fear is to eat. Feeding myself is a basic form of self-reward and a sign of safety and worth.

Another common mechanism is work. Whether we shine shoes, polish cars, wash floors or clean out closets in times of stress, we find these activities help us relax. They are the same behaviors that guaranteed us parental approval in the past.

We also use specific defense mechanisms to manage our fears. I would like to give more attention now to these "subpersonalities."

Most of us are under the illusion that we are one and indivisible when in reality each of us is really a group of personalities. We seldom think of ourselves as made up of different parts, yet inside us there are perhaps a rebel, an intellectual, a seducer, an organizer, each one with its own self-image, body postures, gestures, feelings, words, habits, and beliefs. Each character is a psychological entity, what Roberto Assagioli calls a subpersonality. We can have a multitude of these subpersonalities coexisting as a multitude of lives, all crowded into one person. Often these subpersonalities are far from being at peace with one another.

As Assagioli wrote, "We are not unified; we often feel that we are because we do not have many bodies and many limbs, because one hand doesn't usually hit the other. But metaphorically that is exactly what does happen with us."[2]

I believe that we often have subpersonalities born out of fear and that we need to recognize them so we can step outside of them and observe them. Otherwise, we may believe that one subpersonality is all of us instead of just part of us. Often we allow it far more control than it needs and in this way silence many other parts of ourselves.

A few possible subpersonalities include:

1. *The courageous one* pretends to be courageous so as not to appear afraid;
2. *The snob* fears anyone he or she is not sure of;
3. *The hider* waits for a seeker, someone else to make the first move. I act as if I do not need people, thus pushing them away. When I find myself isolated, I rationalize that others are to blame. "They are selfish; I've got high standards." I am often bitter and aloof. Sometimes I escape into a past period of history into which I would have fitted better.
4. *The strong one* tries to gain the upper hand in all situations. I lack self-confidence and do not know how to build it, so I substitute security by dominating others. Whatever others envy, I always need more of—money, friends, vacations, trips, crayons. I can never relax and enjoy my accomplishments; I am always competing for status.
5. *The good one* wants to dominate others but avoids open competition. My life is based on taboos and my virtue is defined in negative terms. I do not drink, swear, smoke, dance, play cards. I am hypercritical of others, always finding fault. But I am also curious about other people's affairs, especially their morals. I often make people feel guilty and obligated, and try to control their lives "for their own good."
6. *The loving one* clutches at others and uses them in a search for security. Examples would be the man who feels insecure about his masculinity and so exploits women; the husband who never permits his wife to assume an adult role; the mother who does not allow her child to grow up—all in the guise of love.

Learning about the critic

Now I would like to discuss in more detail the most important subpersonality relative to fear, the critic.

Most of the time there is a constant dialogue going on inside us. It is an endless debate with two or more voices arguing whether or not we look good, which article of clothing we should wear; whether or not we should take the job. The voices also discuss important issues such as the meaning of life or our present conduct.

When we listen to these voices we pay more attention to some of them than to others. The positive voices encourage and support us but they seldom speak above a whisper. The negative voices, on the other hand, are very discouraging. Sometimes they are calm and rational and to the point; they keep quiet while we get our work done. At other times they rant and scream, making work impossible. Often the negative voices repeat the same point over and over. "Isn't it time you quit that job?" or "You're too fat. If you only had the will power, you could lose ten pounds."

Negative voices often get the upper hand. They whine and accuse and begin to destroy us because they influence our decisions and drain our energy. Much of this inner dialogue is unconscious, so we are confused and mystified.

However, we need to become aware of these voices in order to restore the balance because they affect the way we live.

Where does the critic come from? It was born in the fear that we would turn our aggression against others and consequently lose their love.

Even the best of parents pass on images of fulfillment, the only ones they know, that force their child to fit in at the expense of the child's individuality. The parents praise the child for conforming or behaving and scold the child for liking or enjoying what the parents feel is unproductive.

The inner dialogue goes something like this. "Father thinks there is something wrong with me because I don't like sports. Father loves me and he is grown up and knows more than I do. He must be right." In order to keep the illusion that I am loved and avoid facing my anger at not being seen or loved for who I really am, I accept the judgment that there must be something wrong with me.

I conspire with father for love but I feel guilty at my anger for not being loved for myself. After a while this critical voice becomes internalized and independent from Father. "There is something wrong with me," and I give up my true feelings.

In turning on ourselves this way, we do penance for our anger at not being loved; for going against our parents; for being different from what they wanted; for betraying their expectations. By punishing ourselves we also hold off the possibility of outside punishment; we lessen the odds of something terrifying happening to us.

The critic's role is to hamper or hurt us before others can, because we fear losing love. We need to realize that the critic is an overgrown bully and much of what it says is bluff. We need to stand up to the critic because it is the single most important obstacle between where we are now and where we want to be. Once we become aware of how the critic operates we will be better able to recognize and label its behavior and then deflate its terrorist image. Our goal is not to eliminate our fear but to rechannel it.

Dealing with our critic

We begin by listening to our inner dialogue. We need to find out who is talking with us, who is for and against us, and what provokes them. We also need to discover whether the government within is a democracy or a dictatorship and which voices have the most power. Then we can listen more to the positive voices, giving them more energy especially in assigning rewards or punishment.

First, however, we need to learn more about out critic, the accumulation of all our enemy voices. The critic is an encyclopedia of all the past self-defeating behaviours that worked so successfully; it maintains an active inventory of our weaknesses and a certain level of misery inside us. It drains our energy so we cannot move ahead.

The critic works under cover and does not fight fair. It makes judgments like, "It's too expensive; I'm too old; I won't have time;

it's foolish; I can't.'' It is especially active in times of crisis and life-challenging debates when opportunities for growth are stronger.

The critic has a long negative memory. It reminds us of every piece of bad news we ever received, of every failing we ever committed. It is a great library of negative information on life.

The critic is also narrow-minded, making generalizations from very few facts and focusing on unimportant details. For instance, whenever you look in the mirror the critic calls attention to your nose, reminding you how big it is.

The critic has fixed ideas about what is right and wrong, and is always on the side of power. It often begins sentences with, ''What if . . .,'' and is basically a coward.

The critic speaks in many voices. Some are frequent, like daily comments about our looks; others are rare, spoken only in crisis times or during the holidays. Each voice has a different level of power and influence. All want us to stay where we are. These negative voices speak from a need for security and safety while the positive voices emphasize action, growth, support, and change. It may help us to identify some of the critic's voices.[3]

The spoiler appears when I am having a good time. During a vacation it reminds me of all the work waiting for me or after my return of everything I forgot to do before I left.

The doubter is always assuring me, ''You'll never be able to do that. It's too difficult for you.'' The doubter has a very low opinion of my abilities and makes me wonder how I can get through the day or if I have any friends at all.

The pessimist predicts bad news. ''There won't be any snow on your ski trip.'' ''You won't enjoy the new job.''

The knife twister does not give me any peace when I have done something wrong. ''How could you do that? Can't you think?''

The nurse tells me not to work too hard, to stay home when I have a headache. The nurse encourages me to be weak and dependent, to avoid responsibilities.

There is one voice that belittles me and turns my ideas, dreams, and accomplishments to ashes. ''So you finally did this. . . . You should have done it years ago.''

Another voice constantly questions whether my friends really care for me. It offers evidence to make me doubt them.

Yet as active and loud as the critic's negative voices are inside me, I need to remember that there are also positive voices.

For instance, the adventurer wants to try something new, the comforter reassures me that I am all right, the chum is a companion and confidant who understands me. The optimist sees the world as ok and considers life to be good. The fan thinks I am special and the go-getter gets things done. Unfortunately I do not always hear these positive voices because the critic is active and speaking in a loud voice.

There are certain areas in my life where the critic is sure to operate. For instance, in dealing with my body image, it loves to magnify my shortcomings and exaggerate unattractive details.

Another favorite area is self-care. If I am uncomfortable being alone, the critic reminds me that loneliness is my fault; if I were more likeable I would not be alone. The critic is sly and can get me to neglect my health, sleep, and need for friends.

In the area of work and play I have the opportunity to speak up for my dreams. The critic is often busy trying to harm my individuality and independence in this area.

The critic does not want me to have loving friends and family. After all, I am unattractive and do not deserve them. Consequently, the critic may encourage me to have friends who are not good for me, who are critical of me and trivialize my interests.

The best defense against the critic is to become aware of the predictable causes and conflict situations in which the critic is likely to appear. The next step is to take more control by becoming a more efficient executive. In this capacity I can inspire teamwork among the voices, maintain order and discipline among them, and assure and encourage fair debate.

As an efficient executive I can pay close attention to scheduling and ensure that every voice is heard. I will make sure that the discussion does not become too one-sided and that no one voice captures all the attention.

A good executive will work to equalize the adversarial voices and make sure they are evenly matched. The critic needs a worthy opponent, not a feeble, newly emerging voice. The executive should also insure feedback for the critic, with every negative comment answered with a positive one, and conflict should be encouraged in a slow rational manner, making sure that issues reach closure without dragging on too long.

The executive part of us needs to put an end to long-running negative tapes. Many times we need simply to admit our errors, make amends, and move on.

Awareness of the critic, therefore, must be joined to mastery in order to move beyond our fears. We need to avoid slipping thoughtlessly into one subpersonality or another. The ability to choose makes a difference similar to that between riding a roller coaster or driving a car.

Fear is harmful only when it controls us, as it can through the subpersonality I have called the critic. In this way fear imposes its ideas and patterns to the exclusion of others.

Our ultimate aim is to increase our sense of self by deepening our acquaintance with our own subpersonalities or different aspects of ourselves. Then instead of disintegrating into a myriad of subpersonalities at war among themselves we can again be one. From our center we can regulate, correct, and care for all the different parts of ourselves without becoming controlled or paralyzed by one part, such as fear.

Endnotes

1. Willard Gaylin, *Feelings* (New York: Ballantine Books, 1984), p. 18.
2. Roberto Assagioli, unpublished lecture notes for course given at the Accademia Tiberina, 1967, p. 2.
3. George Bach and Laura Torbet, *The Inner Enemy* (New York: William Morrow, 1985), p. 91.

Fear and authority in the Church

Brendan P. Riordan

The dynamic of fear • Transition moments •
Developmental factors • Personality types •
Rejection of authority • Images of leadership authority •
Leadership qualities

Reverend Brendan P. Riordan, M.Div., M.S., is director of continuing education for the House of Affirmation. A priest of the diocese of Rockville Centre, New York, Father Riordan holds graduate degrees in psychology and theology. Before joining the staff of the House of Affirmation, Father Riordan served as a parish priest, seminary professor, and diocesan director of church vocations. He is a certified alcoholism counselor, and has lectured widely in the United States and abroad on psychotheological issues. Father Riordan is spiritual advisor to the National Guild of Catholic Psychiatrists, and co-author of Desert Silence: A Way of Prayer for an Unquiet Age.

Somewhere, I read a story about an experience of Pope John XXIII during the first weeks after his election as pope. As he was falling asleep at night, he would review all of the questions and problems in need of decision that had been brought to him during the day, and he would say to himself, "I have to talk to the pope about that in the morning." Then he would stop, think that remark over, and say to himself, "I am the pope. I'll have to talk to God about that in the morning."

It is one of the marks of the Christian community that each member plays a variety of roles. In certain settings, and under certain circumstances, each of us is called upon to exercise a leadership role in the Church. However, in other settings and under other circumstances each of us is subject to someone else's gift of leadership.

Sometimes we fill positions of hierarchical leadership in the Church (as bishops, religious superiors, and pastors), or we exercise the ministerial leadership which characterizes the role of all priests and religious in the Church, or we are subject to leadership in the Church. Because of this variety of roles, each of us must look at and live with authority and leadership "from both sides." We are leaders of the Church, and we are those who are led.

There are many ways to analyze the complex set of relationships created by this variety of roles. I wish to examine with you one particular dynamic which I believe is at work in those relationships, the dynamic of *fear*.

The dynamic of fear

When I speak of fear as an element in these relationships between leaders and those who are led, I mean everything from the simple "jitters" we feel when we have to report to those to whom we are accountable, all the way to the complex resistance and hostility that often characterize these relationships.

It is important to note that fear is something we are born with; it enters into and is part of all our human relationships. In the area of authority and leadership in the Church, the interpersonal aspects of fear, the fear that is part of all our human encounters, is complicated by another kind of fear. No matter what our political or theological position, we all experience, from time to time, a fear that the Church is moving in the wrong direction. This kind of fear is associated with what has come to be called the crisis in leadership. We are anxious about where our leaders are taking us, and whether they have a clear idea of where the Church ought to be going.

I will begin with a simple set of working definitions for some of the words and concepts that are part of the phenomenon I want to describe: fear, anxiety, phobia, and depression.

Fear, in the narrowest and most precise sense of the word, is a physiological and emotional reaction to a particular thing, person, or set of circumstances. The sharp taste of adrenalin in your mouth as you slam on your car brakes to avoid hitting a child who has darted out into the street is the taste of fear. The sweaty palms and cold sensation you feel on your skin as the roller-coaster gets under way are manifestations of fear. The jittery stomach or shaking knees or wavering voice that afflict you when you stand to present an important point at a meeting are all symptoms of fear. In each of these instances, there is a physical and emotional reaction to a particular something, someone, or some circumstance outside of me that is the focus of my feelings. This kind of fear is temporary, or time limited: it begins some time immediately before the encounter with the focus of the fear, and it will end within a reasonable time after the end of the encounter.

Anxiety, on the other hand, is not a temporary or time-limited experience. It is a generalized malaise, characterized by many of the symptoms of fear (such as jittery stomach or other physical ailments), with no particular focus. People who find themselves in an "anxious state" have these symptoms when they wake up in the morning, and these symptoms remain throughout the day. The anxious person may go through each day waiting for some unknown critical and threatening experience, but there is no actual experience powerful enough to justify the anxiety, no experience parallel to "getting off the roller coaster" that can make the fear pass.

Phobias are pathological manifestations of fear, described clinically as "displaced" manifestations of fear and often debilitating. A child who wanders off and gets lost on a beach may develop "agoraphobia" or a fear of open places and become unable to leave the house. But these fears are displaced: the real fear the person is experiencing is the feeling of abandonment and loss of parental love that the child experienced as it wandered alone on that big, open beach. But we think and say so much about how parents love their children that we cannot admit we ever felt abandoned by our parents. So the feelings of terror are transferred from their real focus to some relatively minor circumstantial aspect of the original experience: for the agoraphobe, going out into any open place taps that deep, unconscious reservoir of unspoken—and unspeakable—anxiety about having been abandoned.

In many ways, depression is a fear-related experience that summarizes all the others: it has elements of simple fear, of anxiety, and even of phobia. Setting aside physiological causes, the paralysis of depression is described clinically as "anger turned in on the self." Depression usually develops when some powerful "taboo" or some profound feeling of helplesslessness prevents us from directing deep feelings at their proper object. Widows and widowers, for example, often experience deep depression after the death of a spouse. In many cases, these bereaved partners are unable to deal with feelings of anger at the deceased spouse. Widows and widowers are horrified that they often have feelings best expressed to the deceased as, "How could you leave me!" Since these feelings are "unthinkable," and produce a great deal of guilt, they are deeply repressed. But anger is a powerful emotion, and cannot be disposed of so easily. Deep anger, deeply repressed, redirects and refocuses itself and begins eating away at the angry person who cannot express his or her rage. The symptoms of depression are the manifestation of this anger turned in on the self.

Our encounters with leadership authority often produce some measure of simple fear. But our ongoing relationship with the structure of authority and our concerns about the future of the Church and ourselves sometimes give rise to anxiety and to depression.

Our encounters with authority are productive of fear and anxiety *because of what they imply,* at least *potentially,* about the need to change. A person exercising leadership authority may ask me to change some part of my work, or that person may go so far as to "change me," or "transfer me" to another ministry altogether. On a deeper, and more threatening level, that person may directly or indirectly be asking me to change my vision of the future and my grasp of where the Church is going.

This last fear and anxiety are especially associated with changes in leadership: the election of a new pope or a new general government in a religious community: the arrival of a new pastor or local superior on the scene; or a change of direction signaled by the undertaking of a new program or new policy.

Transition moments

Such transition moments in our lives are often threatening. Since the Second Vatican Council we have lived in a period of transition, and many people are hungering for some kind of stability, some respite from change and experimentation. I am often reminded of something that Winston Churchill said to the English people during the Second World War. Nazi bombers were pounding the country to rubble, and Churchill told his people, "This is not the *end,* nor is it the *beginning* of the end; this is only the *end* of the *beginning."* In that historical context, those words were heroic, and they called the British people to a heroic struggle. In our present ecclesiological context, however, the suggestion that we have only arrived at the "end of the beginning" of change and transition can be exhausting news!

Our ability to deal with transition on the public and institutional level has its roots in how we deal with change and transition in our personal lives. In other words, our ability to respond to leadership and our ability to operate as effective and creative leaders depend on the patterns we have developed for dealing with change and transition throughout our lives.

Here I want to introduce a notion which may at first seem out of place in a discussion of authority and leadership: the notion of intimacy. I want to say that if relationships between Church leaders and those they are responsible to lead are not characterized by intimacy, then those relationships *must* produce fear and anxiety. Furthermore, if those relationships are not characterized by intimacy, they are doomed to fail.

Let me offer a definition of what I mean by intimacy. Intimacy is the capacity to allow myself to be involved with another in such a way that the other person might change me. What is critically important in this notion of intimacy is that I must have a strong sense of my own identity. Let me offer another definition: identity is the basic sense of who I am, the basic grasp that I must have of myself if I am going to allow myself to experience intimacy without fear of losing myself.

Developmental factors

My identity is not a static thing. I grow and change in my ability to grasp myself; I am constantly re-evaluating my development and my identity. Our growth as human persons is marked by our response to the critical transition moments that we encounter in the course of our lives. As young people, we all faced questions like "What am I to do?" "What ideology am I to adopt?" "What occupation shall I undertake?" "What lifestyle shall I choose?" These questions arise for us because we are faced with a variety of options. The question "What ideology am I to adopt?" implies that I am confronted with a variety of persons holding a variety of ideologies, and I feel that I must begin to locate myself somewhere on the range or scale of ideologies presented to me.

These fundamental life choices, the fundamental solutions to these crises of transition, are made in one of two ways. Either I am able to confront the variety before me with some degree of intimacy, allowing the proponents of various ideologies to come close enough to me that I take the risk of having one of them change me, or I withdraw from that risk (fearing that allowing someone to come that close will cause me to lose myself) and take the more superficial course of making an acceptable and safe choice.

Some people can face these crises of transition, and make the commitments that life calls for from time to time because they have risked allowing themselves to grow and change. They have been sure enough of their own fundamental identity that they do not fear losing themselves in the process of opening themselves intimately to other persons. They have periodically re-evaluated themselves, keeping some of what they have become and rejecting some of it. Through the process, however, they have remained in possession of themselves. These people have developed the habit of intimacy; they have developed the interpersonal skill of opening themselves to others.

For some men and women, the prospect of facing these transition crises is intolerable. When they see a crisis coming, they attempt to avoid it: they answer all the questions about themselves at once. They foreclose their identities by making an immediate commitment. This is the case with many people who marry when they are relatively young; it is also what happens with many young people who commit themselves to priesthood or to religious life. They cannot face the crisis of transition and the intimacy it demands; they cannot risk choosing among many alternatives. So they make convenient commitments to things other people value and admire in order to avoid having to re-evaluate themselves and choose an option among alternatives.

For such people, the socially acceptable choice to marry, or the decision to enter upon a career approved and admired by parents and friends—a career like medicine, or the law, or the Church— enables them to establish a satisfactory identity without anguishing over alternatives that threaten to change their identity.

If each of us had to face such a crisis of transition only once in life, the route we took in the decision-making process would make little difference. If our only aim were to make an irrevocable and unreviewable decision, it would matter little whether our choice came from facing the crisis of decision out of our well-developed and courageously re-evaluated grasp of ourselves, or whether we made it on the basis of what we saw as acceptable in order to avoid facing the crisis.

But these crises of transition do not come along once-in-a-lifetime. They present themselves throughout the course of life. The number of people whose marriages end in a few years, who leave priesthood and religious life, and who find themseves in marriages or in religious ministries which cause them deep unhappiness some years after they embark on them, give eloquent testimony to the recurrence of transitional crises. These phenomena show, quite poignantly, that we need to re-evaluate ourselves and our identities periodically at different stages of our adulthood.

Men and women who have faced their fundamental transitional crises out of a strong grasp of their identities, who were not afraid to evaluate and re-evaluate what they had become, who made commitments to particular persons or institutions based on the costly process of allowing themselves to change and grow gradually, are prepared to face life's recurring crises and alternatives out of the same strength.

But people who avoided transitional crises by foreclosing the whole question of their identities, by choosing a lifestyle so they can be protected from life's options, are people whose identities are fragile, brittle, and rigid; life's subsequent crises—the emergence of new questions, new possibilities, and new alternatives—become increasingly more intolerable. Such people find intimacy difficult to achieve because they fear it.

If my grasp of myself is fragile, rooted in a commitment which I made only to avoid facing some basic and fundamental truths about myself and to avoid facing life's alternatives, then the prospect of allowing myself to become involved with another person so deeply that that person might change me is terrifying. If all I have of myself is this fragile and brittle attachment to something I chose almost by default, as a technique for avoiding real choice, then to allow another the power to change me may take away even that small scrap of identity with which I have clothed myself.

People in this situation are like H. G. Wells's Invisible Man. Afraid of not being seen, they have wrapped themselves in the handiest and most acceptable identity they could find, one they could appropriate without great suffering. They do this the way the invisible man wrapped himself in gauze bandages so that people could see the shape and outline of his otherwise invisible form. They fear allowing anyone to change them in any way; they fear that their wrapping of identity will peel away, like the invisible man's bandages, and that there will be nothing left for anyone, including themselves, to see.

If my decision to marry, or to become a doctor or a lawyer, or to embrace a religious vocation, was a step I undertook in order to avoid facing the crisis of my changing identity, then the only identity I have is defined by other people: I am this person's husband or wife, I am a doctor or lawyer or religious or priest as other people, my approving parents, the admiring public, define those roles. If such is the case, then the prospect of allowing you the power to change me is intolerable. If I speak to you honestly and openly, or listen to you so intimately that I allow you to raise questions about my vocation, then I risk having to decide whether I should remain in that vocation. Since I chose my lifestyle in the first place precisely to avoid such a crisis, the possibility of being forced into a recurrence of the crisis is a deadly threat.

On the other hand, persons who faced the transitional crisis squarely at the outset, who went through the painful and risky process of evaluating and re-evaluating themselves, do not fear new crises or new alternatives. Such people chose their lifestyles out of strength, not weakness. They are unafraid of intimacy, because they are unafraid of facing new alternatives. They believe that their fundamental life choices were made for good reasons, and they have the strength that comes from flexibility and the willingness to grow and change.

These considerations are critically important to the relationships between persons in leadership-authority positions in the Church and the persons they lead. If the encounters between such persons are marked by the complex set of responses I have described as "fear" they are, in reality, crises of transition: either the leader is asking the followers to re-evaluate themselves and make new options, or, alternatively, the followers are asking the same thing of their leaders.

The outcome of such encounters depends on how the parties arrived at their positions and on the relative health of their developmental processes. If they are strong enough, if they have developed a sufficiently firm yet flexible grasp of their own identities, then they can face each other with real intimacy, and risk allowing each other the power to bring about change. On the other hand, if the parties have arrived at their present positions by foreclosing their identities so as to avoid real choice, then their identities will be fragile, brittle, and rigid. They will face each other as invisible men or women, both individuals fearing that the other will pick away at the bandages of identity that give their lives their only meaning.

Personality types

Adrian van Kaam has given great attention to this question of the relation between personality development and the structures of leadership authority in the Church. Van Kaam identifies three personality types that affect this relational process:

(1) those who angrily resist and demonize all community structures, and are unable to go beyond them;

(2) those who fanatically deify these structures, and likewise cannot transcend them;

(3) and finally, those who serenely experience and live the community structures as limited but necessary roads toward God and reality.

Van Kaam characterizes the first tendency, the tendency to demonize structure and authority, as receptive personality. These persons are fixated on the level of structureless receptivity, the hallmark of infancy. The infant receives love and attention from its parents; the receptive personality believes that such sweet, unstructured openness should be the goal of all human living. Such people resent any suggestion that they should structure their lives; they present a thick forest of rationalization and intellectualization in favor of a life of sweet, structureless encounter, love, and support. They invite others to regress with them to the unstructured paradise of babyhood buried deep in the unconscious mind. These people demonize structure and authority, and speak in favor of structureless, over-indulgent living.

The second group, those who fanatically deify structure and authority, van Kaam describes as controlling personalities. They are fixated on a somewhat later experience of infancy and early childhood, the need of structure. After babyhood, small children are trained to discipline their needs-fulfillment according to the demands of their environment. Fundamental functions such as eating, drinking, and elimination must be structured according to a prescribed regularity of space and time. Other structures are demanded from children: their waking and sleeping time, the division of the world into touchable and untouchable objects as toys and knives or blankets and electric sockets.

Children at this stage of development have no grasp of the internal value and the unavoidability of structure. They obey and accept structure because of rewards and punishment; they hunger for the kindness bestowed on them by powerful adults when they maintain the required regularity.

In the face of stress and crisis, such persons will regress to the anxious conformity of structure which they lived obsessively and defensively in early childhood. These compulsive-obsessive personalities deify and idolize structure and authority.

The critically important point here is that, whether I deify or demonize authority and structure, I am experiencing them as somehow absolute and ultimate.

Van Kaam's creative personalities, on the other hand, perceive clearly that structure and authority are not at all absolute or ultimate. They are the roads we must walk in order to arrive at the ultimate: knowledge of God and true encounter with reality and the other persons around us. That analysis of van Kaam reminds me of Ghandi's marvelous statement: "There is no path to peace. Peace is the path." The ultimate goal of the Church has nothing to do with structure and authority; the ultimate goal of the Church is neither to perfect structures and authority nor to eliminate them. The ultimate goal of the Church is to ennoble human living here on earth and to bring us all safely into God's Kingdom. Structure and authority are a way, a road to bring us to our ultimate goals. Our experience of human living tells us that without a clear path, we will bump and jostle and bungle our way in every direction; but a road—no matter how rutted and uneven—will draw us together and unite us as fellow-pilgrims and helpmates on the way.

Rejection of authority

Controlling and dependent personalities, regardless of whether they deify or demonize structures of authority, attach an inordinately high degree of importance to authority. Richard Sennett, in his book *Authority,* explores what he describes as the building of the master-servant bond under the guise of rejection of authority.[1]

It is Sennett's contention that the process of rejecting authority is often the device used by persons subject to authority to make living with their genuine desire for dependence both acceptable and tolerable. He describes three mechanisms for accomplishing this:

disobedient dependence, printing a positive, ideal image of authority from the negative image which exists, and a fantasy about the disappearance of authority.

To describe the first mechanism, disobedient dependence, Sennett offers the case history of a woman he calls Helen Bowen. Helen was a woman in her middle twenties, raised in a middle-class Irish family in Boston. Helen was constantly quarrelling with her parents over the fact that she was romantically involved with a black man.

Sennett describes Helen's behavior pattern as disobedient dependence and suggests that she used her defiance to erect a barrier that made it safe for her to taste the pleasures of dependence. As long as her involvement with "unsuitable" men caused bickering, she felt it safe to be in her parents' home and to take advantage of the leisure and security they provided. When they approved of her life, however, she resisted being with them, fearing she would lose her identity and appear to be dependent on them.

Helen might seem to be rebelling against parental authority by her choice of romantic partners, but, in fact, she was rebelling within authority. She was disobeying, but her parents were unknowingly regulating the terms of her obedience and disobedience because she planned her actions with reference to their preferences. In fact, her behavior can be characterized as compulsive disobedience: she discovers her parents' preferences, and then does the opposite. This compulsive disobedience has nothing to do with independence and autonomy. In fact, Helen depended on her parents' disapproval in order to make it safe for her to enjoy her reliance on them and on their strength.

Her relationship to the clinic's therapists is a further indication of what she was looking for. First she asked for medication, then she complained that it was too weak, although she failed to use it as prescribed. Finally she demanded a new therapist because she felt the first one "gave in too easily" to her request for meds. In this set of transactions she is outlining her true feelings about authority and strength. She asks the question, "Who is strong enough to take care of me?" and she proposes her own answer to the question: "Someone who is strong enough to oppose me." As she only feels safe allowing her parents to take care of her if they oppose her choice of lovers, so she only feels safe allowing a therapist to take care of her if the therapist is strong enough to oppose her in a similar way. Helen sets up that opposition by her disobedience, so she can safely enjoy the security of dependence.

Sennett's second mechanism for building the master-servant bond under the guise of rejection of authority is what he calls "printing a positive, ideal image of authority from the negative image which exists." He characterizes this mechanism as *idealized substitution.*

Again, Sennett turns to a case study to illustrate his point. He describes an accounting office where there was a great deal of tension in the relationships between the supervisor and her staff of accountants. The staff felt that their supervisor was "a flunky," always playing up to her own superiors, and that she gave them no real direction or supervision. They complained, in other words, that she did not drive them hard enough to accomplish really satisfying professional goals. With a kind of converse complementarity, the supervisor felt that her staff was composed of childish and unrealistic persons.

Interestingly, the members of this department's staff had all transferred into this division, and they admitted that they had done so because the office had the reputation for being easy and undemanding. When asked if they would care to transfer out to other divisions, where the supervisors were known to be more rigid and demanding, each member of the staff rejected the proposal immediately.

Here we have people rejecting authority quite vehemently, but allowing the authority figure to control the transaction completely. For them the answer to "What is good authority?" is simple: "Good authority is everything that our supervisor is not."

In the first place, then, the staff members in that office developed both their definition of authority and the absolute rejection of it with reference to the person actually in authority. Sennett uses an analogy from photography: the person in authority is like the negative image a camera produces; the definition of what would be

good in the exercise of authority is developed by printing this negative image, and the resultant print will be, in every detail, the
positive or the precise opposite of the negative image of the actual,
existing situation.

The powerful negative feelings that supervisor and staff had for
each other locked them into each other's lives. By their mutual rejection, they became bonded to each other.

Finally, Sennett describes what he calls "a fantasy about the
disappearance of authority." The key wish statement of those subject to authority in this unconscious bonding device is the statement, "Everything would be all right if only the people in charge
would disappear."

This position is the ultimate of printing a positive image of
authority from the negative; it suggests that the only positive image
possible is a blank print. If no one were in charge, things would be
better than they are with these people in charge. Perhaps this rather
subtle mechanism brings us closest to understanding what Sennett
is getting at in talking about building the master-servant bond by
rejecting authority. To go all the way in the process of rejecting
authority, all the way to envisioning the disappearance of authority, is to face the chaos of an unstructured world. It brings us face-
to-face with the satisfying rush of feelings associated with the final
rejection of authority and with our terror at the thought of being
leaderless.

In each of Sennett's three scenes or mechanisms, then, the final
outcome is the realization that the rejection of authority creates or
strengthens the bond between the leader and those who are led.

Images of leadership authority

So far we have been looking at the ways that our developmental
deficiencies and our fears cause us to relate to authority in unhealthy and unproductive ways. It should be clear that these considerations affect us both as leaders and as people who are led. The
fears and mechanisms make it difficult for us to relate to those who
are in positions of leadership authority over us, and they make it

equally difficult for us to relate to those over whom we exercise leadership authority.

Now I would like to speak more positively by drawing some conclusions about the nature of leadership authority, and making a few suggestions about dealing successfully with it.

Let us look, first, at the word authority itself. It has its etymological root in the Latin word *auctor* which means author or originator. This original Latin sense suggests that authority is productive, and that persons in authority are supposed to guarantee to others that there is lasting value in what they do. This view of authority emphasizes the role of the leader as a creative person.

In contrast to this positive view of leadership authority, we generally use the concepts of authority and power interchangeably. How did a word which was meant, originally, to describe a life-giving and liberating reality come to be associated with a word like power, with such pejorative connotations today?

Our perceptions of authority have been shaped by history, culture, and psychological predispositions. Our culture and history offer us three general categories for understanding authority:

(1) the traditional model of authority is based upon beliefs established by long-standing tradition;

(2) the legal model is rooted in the belief that there is "legitimacy" to the rule-making process in society, and there is "legality" to the rules coming out of that process, giving certain rights to those who occupy posts of command;

(3) The charismatic model draws its authority from the extraordinary devotion of the followers to their leader because of the leader's special "sacredness" or force of personality.

Freud and others tell us that our perception and images of authority are formed in childhood. Integrated adults, according to Freud, come to recognize the limits as well as the strengths of their parents. Unhealthy reactions to authority, such as fear or passive-aggressive behavior, occur in individuals who were only able to see their parental figures as all-powerful and threatening. Such people, when they were children, perceived their parents as rigid persons whose discipline was erratic or difficult to understand. This perception is then projected on to other authority figures who are viewed as frightening alter-parents. It is our responsibility to examine and understand our image of our leaders, and the factors which motivate our reactions to them. At the same time, we also have the responsibility of examining the models of leadership authority we project when we function as leaders.

Let us look at two familiar models of leadership which are basically power-oriented, in the pejorative sense.

The first is the *paternal* leader. People who exercise this form of leadership have often convinced themselves of their good intentions. This Father-knows-best attitude is based on the belief that power and maturity belong to the leader alone. The followers who accept this leadership model are willing to trade off their dignity as the acceptable price for being cared for. But, besides fostering unhealthy dependence in the followers, paternalism will eventually cause confusion and anxiety in the leader. When signs of independence arise within the group, the leader reacts, first, to what is perceived as ingratitude ("What more do you want from me?"), and then to betrayal ("After all I've done for you!")

Paternalism eventually destroys because it is based on five obvious distortions of the truth:

(1) the leader is not a father or mother;

(2) the members of the group are not children;

(3) the group members do not enjoy the face-to-face intimacy which should characterize "fatherly" relations;

(4) the leader cannot really offer what the group most hopes for—parental care;

(5) finally, and worst of all, paternalistic leaders, unlike good parents, need to have their followers remain children.

The second power-oriented model of leadership is the *autonomous* leader. Beginning with the feeling that "You need me; I don't need you," these self-proclaimed experts deny all reciprocal social power, and demand unilateral power instead. Because autonomous leaders are convinced that they are self-sufficient, they are unaware of the basis of true strength: that we are strong together, and that the group, far from diminishing the strength of the leader, enhances it. Autonomous leaders exercise their authority with the same basic, fatal flaw as paternalistic leaders: neither kind of leader allows the group to grow.

These abuses of authority occur so often because we have a tendency to make an idol of authority when we see it as power. When we turn authority into a thing or an end in itself we are easily seduced by its common illusions. Here are five of the lies we often accept when we forget that authority has as its central purpose creative service for others rather than power over subjects:

(1) authority is a possession of the leader;

(2) authority is not accountable;

(3) authority is a privilege that offers its possessors special status;

(4) obedience is a virtue for followers only; and

(5) obedience is a passive virtue: being grateful, deferential, and docile.

So at times, what we view as disobedience has genuine obedience at its core.

Finally, as a closing observation about the nature of leadership authority, it is important to note that a leader is not so much a person who does things right, as a person who finds the right things to do. If we see leadership in terms of doing things right, then we are talking about management, not leadership. If we ask only, "What are the right things to do?" and not the more basic questions, "Whom are we serving?" and "For what reasons are we serving them?" then our efforts and our energy may be spent on what we think others need rather than on what is truly needed.

Leadership qualities

I promised a few minutes ago that I would start talking "more positively," and now I believe I am ready to do that.

When I think of leaders, I think of persons who present themselves as models that others will want to emulate. If we are Church leaders who look exhausted, burnt out, and discouraged, we do not offer an attractive model for anyone to follow. Our actions, our appearance, and our expressed values need to encourage and enliven our communities.

Leaders need to identify, promote, and defend the best attitudes and values shared by group members.

What are the qualities of leadership? First and foremost, leadership needs to be grounded in intimacy. It must be aware of the possibility of changing the lives of others and at the same time be open to the risk of being changed by them.

Leadership needs also to be grounded in trust: a firm conviction about the goodness of those who call us to point out the proper way.

Leadership needs to be grounded in a readiness to listen: to see and admit that none of us has a monopoly on the mysterious movements of the Holy Spirit.

Leadership needs to be grounded in a willingness to innovate: recognizing that human society is constantly changing and that we must respond to the newer needs and challenges that these fluid times offer us.

Finally, leadership needs to be grounded in a willingness to be creative, even in ways that might seem risky and dangerous.

The leadership we need today must also bear the hallmarks of availability, accountability, and vulnerability. Finally, and in some ways most importantly, leadership implies caring and being genuinely concerned about the whole community: about those who lead and those who are led.

In the long run, no one can say more about overcoming fear than John: "Perfect love drives out fear" (I John 4:18). What an unusual and provocative way of describing love and fear! Love is not the opposite of hatred; love is the opposite of fear. Fear is not the opposite of courage; fear is the opposite of love. Authority is not the opposite of subjection; authority is the opposite of powerlessness; and the power that underlies authority is the power of love. If we are capable of intimacy, then we are capable of dealing with authority exercised by others or ourselves. If we are capable of real intimacy, then authority, the gift of God to the whole community, will enable each of us to live and work in peace, security, and real liberty.

Mother Theresa of Calcutta has spoken beautifully about the attitude we should have toward God's limitless power and authority: "Give God permission!" She means that God, though limitless in power, respects our freedom and waits with loving patience for us to step forward in faith and courage to offer ourselves. When we have done this, God will do wonders through us.

There could be no better summary of what it means to use and to respect authority. We must give our leaders permission to love us, and to be loved by us. If we can do that, we will liberate them from their misconceptions about power and from our misplaced dependence. In the end, we will have liberated each other for our journey to the Kingdom.

Endnotes

1. Richard Sennett, *Authority* (New York: Alfred A. Knopf, 1980).

Whom should I fear?

Martel Bryant
Bernard J. Bush

Avoiding fear • Evan's experience •
Refusing to face fear • Accepting fear •
Fearing God • Transforming fear • Fear of the Lord

Martel Bryant, M.D., is psychiatric consultant to the House of Affirmation in Montara, California, and maintains a number of clinical and teaching posts in the San Francisco Bay Area. He has a special interest in individual psychoanalytic psychotherapy and the significance of loss and grieving in our lives.

Reverend Bernard J. Bush, S.J., Ph.D., director of the Montara House of Affirmation, is a member of the California Province of the Society of Jesus. Father Bush studied theology at Regis College, Willowdale, Ontario, and received his doctoral degree from Saybrook Institute in San Francisco, California. He served as student chaplain at the University of San Francisco, and later as spiritual director at the Jesuit theologate in Berkeley, California. After interning in pastoral psychology at Boston State Hospital, he joined the staff of the House of Affirmation and opened its Boston consulting center. Father Bush has been active in the directed retreat movement, written numerous articles concerning spirituality and social justice, and has lectured on Ignatian spirituality, religious life, mental health, and social justice.

At first glance, fear seems to hold a modest position in how we understand and help people psychologically. In the Christian theological sense, fear appears to be defined narrowly. Considering this human emotion from the perspective of both psychology and theology enriches our understanding. We see that defenses against fear have obscured its important role in human development and hidden some important distinctions between bravado and courage, and despair and hope in our spiritual lives.

Fear is one of the most common, painful, and important of all human emotions. It is also usually overlooked. We are prone to be ashamed of our fears and to hide them even from ourselves. We bury them deeply, disguise the burial site, then forget we were ever in that part of the forest. When mental health professionals hide their fear, they fail to consider the role of fear in human development, suffering, psychopathology, healing, and spirituality.

Avoiding fear

Psychiatrists, for instance, will acknowledge readily that they work with people about painful feelings, usually anxiety and depression. But they are less inclined to describe the sources of these emotions. Mental health workers will talk about counseling for "grief work." But few inquire about the outcomes and processes of that grief work. In ego psychology, the formation of conscience and ego ideals is considered a massive developmental step. However, the dynamic growth of the ego ideals, the maturing of the conscience, or the role of spirituality in this process, is hardly mentioned. How do we place ourselves in emotional relation with our history, our family, and our culture? How do we come to an adult concept and love of our God? These questions have eluded psychology theorists, in part we believe, because there is fear in the answers.

According to the old English root words for fear in Webster's Dictionary, fear is not a stranger. It is a spy which comes upon us as a bandit in ambush, overwhelming our wish to hide from it. Do you remember your own childhood fears: fear of being abandoned, of the dark, of animals, of ghosts, of spiders or snakes? Many of us have forgotten those old familiar fears, but all of us had them. In the second five years of our life we became concerned about injury or death to ourselves or those we loved. We began to question and wonder. We also learned to hide and seek fear and become adept at hiding it.

Fear is the conscious emotional apprehension of our mortal limits. It usually comes upon us suddenly whenever some immediate, palpably threatening circumstance overwhelms us. It is the car hurtling at you, blood flooding from the mouth of the stranger stricken next to you, the body of your parent or dear friend or child grown cold. Even to talk about fear generally and theoretically is to hide its impact and meaning. Here is an example drawn from the experience of someone close to one of us (M. Bryant).

Evan's experience

In April 1984, my son Evan was a big, bright, mostly fearless two and a half year old recognizably within the normal developmental limits for that charming and exasperating age. One warm Tuesday afternoon my wife was reading a newspaper beside the hot-tub as Evan and his brother Kenneth splashed and played in and around it. She was startled suddenly by a worried Kenneth, "Look, Mom, Evan is trying to swim underwater." When she reached the tub the little boy was inert, floating face down. She hauled him out of the water pale, cool, unconscious, not breathing. As a CPR instructor, she had him over her knee expressing out the water in seconds. Shortly he began to sputter, then to gasp and choke and cry. His mother wrapped him and held him and soon his color returned. To the best of our knowledge he had no physical damage as a consequence of this event. His development continued on an expressive, affectionate, aggressive track. Occasionally, in the year that followed he would talk about the time that he "died."

We parents seemed to have more trouble with the event. We would wake at night with the image of his lifeless body floating in the tub and shiver with anguish. A year later we joined a swim club and enrolled him in a two-student swim class with a buddy who had a backyard pool. Evan was interested at first, but as the classes proceeded he became progressively resistant. At first he let the instructor hold him in the deep water; later he cried and refused to go into water over his head. He begged us to stop the lessons. Frightened about the consequence of stopping, we persisted. Evan, losing trust in us, became more frightened. He would plead, "I hate this day. Let's not go to the club today." At the same time he tried desperately to overcome his fear. As the impasse continued his fear spread. He became a fretful, self-doubting, clinging child; his sleep and appetite were disturbed. He became anxious about many things, stayed indoors more, and regressed to levels of play he had outgrown. He could not tolerate being far away from his mother very long. On July 4, the day a swim party was planned at his buddy's house, matters came literally to a head. Evan awoke crying with a severe headache. Taking him to the pediatrician, I was struck by how uneasy he was leaving the house and his mother. "Why do I have to go? What will he do to me?" The gentle pediatrician found nothing organically wrong with Evan to account for the headache except that his blood pressure was elevated. "Is he worrying about something?"

Finally we faced our own harmful fear. "It's all right, Evan. You can go in the water when you want and the way you want." In the days following he discovered fun in jumping into his mother's arms in the deep water. He was delighted with himself and the symptoms disappeared. He became our bouncy, loveable, risk-taking, competitive Evan again. What had happened to Evan? Was he anxious, depressed, regressed, psychophysiologic, suffering from a separation disorder or emotional crisis? To all of the above we might answer yes. But we know something deeper. He was afraid.

Refusing to face fear

We can see more easily in a young child what may be hidden in our adult life. A client of ours in her middle years was depressed over unresolved grief concerning the recent death of her parents. As the work of mourning progressed in therapy her depression cleared, but she discovered a new problem. A deeply committed religious, she was ashamed to admit that, brought close by her grief, she was frightened by the prospect of her own death. In another instance, a priest was puzzled by a series of compulsive behaviors which invariably defeated him whenever he got close to achieving something important. We began to make real headway only when we got in touch with memories of a cruel and sadistic parent who was unconsciously still regulating and defeating his life. These stories, where psychological work discloses an underlying crippling fear, are repeated often in our work at the House of Affirmation.

However realistic and adult we like to think ourselves, we are often whistling in the dark. We wall off a threatening world which happens to *other* people, not us, or if to us, then at another time. In our hearts we tend to feel omnipotent and immortal and (soon-to-be) living happily ever after. Neurotic symptoms of various kinds are further examples of the compromises we make with a painful reality. When we are anxious we express the feeling of fear but we refuse to face the source of the fear. Our phobias are symbolic targets of our more basic fears. Elevators, heights, crowds frighten us, but the underlying source remains hidden. When we are depressed we are often submitting to the judgments of a fearing and fearful conscience, but the source of the fear remains obscure to our conscious minds.

There is a process that we do not understand by which we become transformed. In this transformation we are at once more mature, more distinctively unique, and more clearly placed in relationship with those we love, with our history, our culture, and our God. We might call this process a miracle. Psychology has no name for it, but it relates to concepts of identification and identity. Identification means something new taken from experience with someone else has been added to ourselves. Identity is when the "somethings new" are put into an integrated whole. The psychologist might call this transformation, separation and identity formation. Thus labeling these components of a larger dynamic field overlooks relationship aspects, integrative activities, and feeling states essential to the process. Such labeling also hinders study or description of how this formation takes place. Emotional growth or maturation is a more comprehensive term but too global and generalized. Character formation comes close, but psychology has no theory for character development. This growth is a largely silent process more dramatic and visible at crisis points when we are unprepared to meet a life transition. Silent or otherwise, this growth is always painful.

Accepting fear

When our defenses are overridden and our narcissistic complacency is disturbed we feel fear. Fear hurts and alerts. We may then move to avoid or consciously accept fear. If we accept the feeling we become aware that some aspect of ourselves and our lives is coming to an end. We have to die, to give up something, to change ourselves and our view of the world, our beliefs, hopes, values, relations with others and with God. We experience this awareness as loss and grief: my life ends here; her life, his life ends there. This hope is dead, that promise faded. So we mourn the Eden we dreamed of as we find and yield to the life we have. We cannot mourn alone; we must share the process. Under the best circumstances we mourn with someone who has walked our path of grief, known our fear, accepted the loss, acquired some of the new skills, capacities, understanding, and beliefs which help them and us to a new view. With them we may first painfully try on our new requirements, imitate and modify and identify. When the transition is made internally, we are transformed. Our ego ideals have been modified, elaborated, and interrelated. Our conscience functions less arbitrarily and punitively, and more comprehensively. We see ourselves and the world in a different way. We have taken into ourselves qualities derived from the substance of what we lost and placed ourselves in more realistic and continuous relation with it. Evan's fearless omnipotence in the water changed as the trauma and pattern of his mastery of fear transformed him. Those patterns included play with his mother (with whom he "died") that induced new experiences in their relationship and new skills in swimming. (These experiences in turn will be internalized and preserved in patterns of risk-taking, play, and subsequent skill development in his life journey.) This step of the process ends in comfort and love, a sense of being more, a sense of wholeness, of knowing who we are, of what is important and how we relate to the world, and through the world, spiritually to God.

Since death is the ultimate and final threat to our well-being, the end of our future and our hopes, we fear it most. In fact, all intermediate threats and their attendant fears take their strength from the fear of death. The scale of fearlessness can be measured by how near to death itself any threat is perceived to be. Death is the horizon of our life since it is the end of it. For those without further belief, death is *absolute,* since it is the only certainty in our future. All else is conjecture. We can more or less confidently assume that we will survive reading this chapter. But our assumption is not a certainty. Only death is certain and absolute, and all other intermediate fears take their power from that reality.

For those of us who believe in eternal life, the horizon of life has moved through and beyond death. Eternal life provides the horizon and absolute future against which we measure death and all the intermediate fears we feel. Life with God is our destiny. So Paul exclaims, "O death, where is your sting?" (1 Cor. 15:55). When we realize that death is not the ultimate evil or the absolute future we can master our fears and not be overcome by them.

Our unreflective human consciousness is frequently self-deceitful. Most of us live with an unacknowledged sense of immortality and omnipotence, as Evan did before he "died." We believe that we will not die, and thus we rival God. We create our own horizon beyond death by denying its reality. This self-deception is shattered from time to time when we realize that we are going to die, that we are not immortal. This experience occurs more frequently as we grow older, often accompanied by a chill, or a sense of dread or fear. It involves the shattering of an illusion. We are jarred into a certain truth.

Fearing God

There are times when we fear God as a threat to our well-being or as a supreme punisher. Spiritual writers call this a servile fear, a kind of quivering dread in the presence of our self-constructed image of God. When we picture God that way, we are in fact bringing God within the horizon of death, as an ally of death, and part of the absolute threat that death is for unbelievers. We envision God as a creature of time, bounded by the same limits we experience. Our faith tells us that God is the ally of life, not death, and that he beckons us from beyond death to join him there. That hope is our corrective to fear, since both hope and fear are attitudes toward the future. Fear sees the end of the future at death, hope looks through to eternal life.

God's promise of eternal life is absolute and irrevocable from his side, but conditional on our cooperation with his designs. We must live so as to make the hope plausible. A virtuous life is necessary to manage and master our fears. The absolute good is to be with God after death. The absolute disaster is to lose God. This kind of fear of the Lord is indeed "the beginning of wisdom" (Ps. 111:10). Moreover, Jesus has shown us that the way to such wisdom is by embracing death and its attendant fears, not by avoiding them. Remember his invitation, "Take my yoke upon your shoulders and learn from me, for I am gentle and humble of heart. Your souls will find rest, for my yoke is easy and my burden light" (Matt. 11:29, 30).

He further reminds us, "If a man wishes to come after me, he must deny his very self, take up his cross, and begin to follow in my footsteps. Whoever would save his life will lose it, but whoever loses his life for my sake will find it" (Matt. 16:24, 25). The essential process for the Christian is the passion, death, and resurrection of Christ, ritualized in the liturgy and the Blessed Sacrament.

For religious, the vows of poverty, chastity, and obedience imply a closer identification with Christ in his paschal mystery. The vows have been described as a kind of death, a foregoing of what this world cherishes and values. The vowed life makes possible that single-hearted witness to the truth of the things of the Lord beyond death. That state of mind and heart allows men and women religious to be free from worries and fears, particularly those which arise from attachments and the consequent fear of loss. It is possible, for example, that the rich young man who approached the Lord feared what life would be like without the security of his wealth.

One positive outcome of this painful process is maturation and affirmation resulting from the mastery of fear. There are, however,

many other possibilities. Unprepared persons under the wrong circumstances will retreat from fear, deny the actualities that frighten
them as Evan did, and develop ways of hiding from life. They will
project their inner fears out onto the world, and live life pretending
and compromising. To the extent they do this, they impair their
potential and increase their vulnerability to fear. The architects of
programs that propagandize or "brain wash" people recognize the
importance of fear. Persons held hostage often inadvertently identify with their captor or their captor's beliefs. Crisis theory in
psychology holds that development is not continuous but occurs at
intervals around periods of fear, confusion, and unsettlement.
However, crisis theory does not go far enough in facing the importance of fear or describing the processes of mastering it. Psycho-
therapists aim to uncover the compromises which self-deception,
symptoms, and character stereotyping create for them and their
clients and to reach the genuine sources and solutions of fear.

Therapists often fear needed empathic identification with their
clients. They need to look for therapeutic methods that take these
goals and fears into account. Such a perspective requires a shift
from the stereotyped and defensive view of therapist (or helper) as
an uninvolved knower and interpreter of truth. It speaks to a
shared exploration with an empathic awareness of the fear for each
of us that accompanies every defense and every motive. It emphasizes relationship, shared goals, safety, empathy, and the importance of love and heart. It is a challenge to find within the means to
master a painful reality. These means are often made vivid in treatment by transference/counter-transference, the use of transitional
objects, play, risk-taking, and identification. Evan's growth re-
sumed when his parents could understand his fear and their own
enough to provide a setting of trust for him.

Transforming fear

What values of a psychotherapist can set the context for these
goals and methods? They include a willingness to be transformed,
and to experience the frightening pulls and tugs of being a transitional and transferential object for and with patients: dying, living,

and dying again. Margery Williams writes of these values in *The Velveteen Rabbit:*

> "What is REAL?" asked the Rabbit one day, when they were lying side by side near the nursery fender, before Nana came to tidy the room. "Does it mean having things that buzz inside you and a stick-out handle?"
>
> "Real isn't how you are made," said the Skin Horse. "It's a thing that happens to you. When a child loves you for a long, long time, not just to play with, but REALLY loves you, then you become Real."
>
> "Does it hurt?" asked the Rabbit.
>
> "Sometimes," said the Skin Horse, for he was always truthful. "When you are Real you don't mind being hurt."
>
> "Does it happen all at once, like being wound up," he asked, "or bit by bit?"
>
> "It doesn't happen all at once," said the Skin Horse. "You become. It takes a long time. That's why it doesn't often happen to people who break easily, or have sharp edges, or who have to be carefully kept. Generally, by the time you are Real, most of your hair has been loved off, and your eyes drop out and you get loose in the joints and very shabby. But these things don't matter at all, because once you are Real you can't be ugly, except to people who don't understand."[1]

What criteria can we employ in any helping relationship to determine how successfully we are contending with fear in the other and ourselves? The sense of trust and of integrity within the relationship is certainly important and often mentioned. When fears are faced and understood, the situation will have a sense of immediacy, accessibility, vividness, and depth of connection between partners.

The reader will recognize that the processes we are considering are important because they occur not only in spiritual or emotional crises, but daily throughout our lives. Attention to fear in the other and ourselves affects all significant relationships. Thus, whatever our role, be it sister, brother, father, mother, nurse, physician, confessor, spiritual adviser, formation director, or program administrator, we must face and overcome the fears which warp and distort our perceptions and those of others.

Fear is not the only painful emotion with which mental health professionals must deal. However, fear is strikingly elusive, subject to repression, projection, isolation, intellectualization, and denial. In the past, the presence of fear has been insufficiently recognized in our clients, ourselves, our theories of development and of therapy.

There are some important differences in the understanding, goals, and methods of working with people when we consciously take fear into account. Today, Evan is enthusiastically on track in his development. He and his parents have learned better ways to deal with their fear of drowning. But the fear will certainly re-appear in more elaborate and disguised ways at points of stress through Evan's life. At the House of Affirmation, we are learning to listen more keenly for fear in our clients and ourselves. In order to do so, we have to attend to some professional theoretical blinders. We hide from our fear of death by *feeling* it could not happen to us, and *thinking* it will not happen to us soon. Similarly, we evade fear by assigning therapeutic tasks such as doing grief work, or coping with anxiety or depression. We isolate these tasks from the larger frightening developmental picture and so reduce our usefulness. This important larger picture is character development in the good sense of the term. In this process adults are transformed from primitive, narcissistic, isolated, role-playing individuals to more mature and genuinely connected people finding comfort in relationships to family, societies, culture, and God's world. The means by which this transformation takes place include fearing, grieving, and successful identification with those who offer mastery of fear. For Christians this is often through Christ and spiritual companions. Within this context spirituality is not an isolated dimension of our lives, but an integral way through fear and grief to reach our transformation in God. It is a goal and a choice. The alternative is arrested development: hiding from the knowledge of life and death by retreating emotionally into fantasy, and becoming isolated, frightened observers of life.

Fear of the Lord

Whom should we fear? Certainly we should fear ourselves, and our capacity to hide from our fears. Whom *should* we fear? God, to whom and with whom we may grow and find our own substantial and fearfully finite being. The felt and acknowledged relation of that finite being, ourselves, to the infinite God, is called Fear of the Lord, a gift of the Holy Spirit. This fear of God is different from that described earlier which is based on reducing God to human size and consequently dreading him. This healthy fear is based on the sure knowledge of God's love for us, and his faithfulness to his promises, the source of our hope. This love is filial rather than servile love. V. R. A. Tanquerey, in his classic, *The Spiritual Life,* describes the gift of Fear of the Lord in somewhat archaic language.

> The gift of fear perfects the virtues of hope and temperance. It perfects the former by inspiring us with a fear of displeasing God and of being separated from Him. It perfects the latter by detaching us from the pleasure that could bring about separation.
>
> Hence, it may be defined as a gift which inclines our will to a filial respect for God, removes us from sin [sic], displeasing to Him, and gives us hope in the power of His help.[2]

The gift of Fear of the Lord helps us keep our priorities straight. It focuses our lives beyond death, and strengthens us to face the tasks of our life here on earth. The psalmist expresses that relationship of the here and the hereafter in the light of our fears in a way that has encouraged countless people through the ages.

> The Lord is my shepherd; I shall not want.
> . . . .
> Even though I walk in the dark valley
>   I fear no evil; for you are at my side
> With your rod and your staff
>   that give me courage.
>
> Psalm 23:1, 4

What better statement could we have of the need to master the fears that arise from the dark valleys of our lives? What better way to express the source of courage and confidence that makes such mastery possible? We will inevitably fear the evils lurking in the dark valleys if we disbelieve. That is, either we will think that the dark valley is an absolute reality and we will experience fright, dread, or even terror, or that we are alone in the valley dependent on our own resources without a rod or staff to lean on. Either view represents a failure of hope and allows the fear of harm or death to close off our future.

But it is impossible for us humans once and for all to so confidently lean on the rod and the staff that we never fear again. The near drowning of Peter is an illustration: note how Peter alternates between fear and confidence. We pick up the story as the terrified disciples in a storm-tossed boat see Jesus walking on the water.

> Jesus hastened to reassure them: "Get hold of yourselves! It is I. Do not be afraid!" Peter spoke up and said, "Lord, if it is really you, tell me to come to you across the water." "Come!" he said. So Peter got out of the boat and began to walk on the water, moving toward Jesus. But when he perceived how strong the wind was, becoming frightened, he began to sink and cried out, "Lord, save me!" Jesus at once stretched out his hand and caught him. "How little faith you have!" he exclaimed. "Why did you falter?" Once they had climbed into the boat, the wind died down. (Matt. 14:27-32)

This story richly illustrates the psychological experience of alternating between fear based on imminent danger and assurance based on trust. When we enter the dark valley, or in this case the threatening water, leaning on the staff of the Lord does not make the threat go away. It is our horizon that changes. We are enabled to look beyond the danger that inspires fear. But when we falter because of little faith, the terror returns. For a moment, Peter forgot that he was depending on Jesus and thought that he was walking on the water on his own. When that grandiose illusion of immortality was shattered by the raging storm and the realization of danger, Peter began to sink. At that point he re-established contact with Jesus and was safe once again.

The parallels between that incident and Evan's drowning and subsequent attempts to master his fear are striking. At first Evan trusted his instructor, then grew fearful again; later he trusted his mother, and his fears diminished. The process of mastering fear is just such a fluctuation between confident trust and hope, and the reawakening of fear. Both stories illustrate our lifetime task of mastering our fears by maintaining confidence in a security beyond the danger. Evan trusted his mother. We need to depend on God's will and the gift of the Holy Spirit, fear of the Lord.

Endnotes

1. Margery Williams, *The Velveteen Rabbit* (Philadelphia, Penn.: Running Press, 1981), pp. 14, 16.
2. V. R. Adolphe Tanquerey, *The Spiritual Life,* Herman Branderis, trans., second revised edition (Westminster, Md.: Newman, 1948), p. 623.

Fear of the evening shadows

Marie Kraus

Fear of aging • The experience of growing older •
Guidelines for coping • Loving ourselves •
Broadening our world • Role models • A bright future

Sister Marie Kraus, S.N.D.deN., M.A., director of media for the House of Affirmation and executive editor of Affirmation Books, is a member of the Boston Province of the Sisters of Notre Dame de Namur. She pursued her undergraduate studies at Emmanuel College, Boston, and graduate studies at Boston University. Before joining the staff of the House of Affirmation, Sister Kraus had a wide variety of work experience, including teacher on the elementary, secondary, and college levels, secretary to the manager of a manufacturing plant, college administrator, province communications coordinator, and ghost writer. She is a member of several professional organizations including Women in Communication.

Most of us can remember being afraid of the dark when we were children. We feared the dark night outside when we were safe in the house, and we feared the dark under the bed or in the closet when we were safe under the bedcovers.

One small boy filled with this fear kept calling down to his mother for reassurance. Finally the mother declared, "Now God is with you and your guardian angel and your patron saints. You don't need to be afraid of the dark." The boy responded, "I know God and my guardian angel and my patron saints are here, but I want someone with some skin on."

We may smile recalling our childhood fears. But as we mature we often grow to fear a different kind of darkness—that of the evening shadows of old age, retirement, and death. As young people we seldom think of these matters: they are too far in the future. But little by little they begin to touch our lives, and our thoughts turn to them more frequently.

When the speakers for the symposium on fear sent in the titles and descriptions of their papers, I noticed that while they chose important aspects of fear, no one selected fear of aging and retirement. For many people these fears are pressing, and so I will focus on them in this chapter.

My own awareness of aging began soon after I entered a religious community one February during pre-Vatican II days. My mother visited me once a month. During the cold weather we sat indoors and while my mother removed her coat, she never took off her hat. Finally in May we went outdoors to walk around the grounds. A gentle breeze tugged at the brim of my mother's hat so she removed it. I remember I caught my breath with a pang of regret as I saw how her hair had grayed in those few months from February to May. The fear of aging touched me for the first time. I felt the coming loss of my mother, although she did not die until thirty years later.

Fear of aging

Why do we instinctively fear aging? It is a natural process: we begin to age as soon as we leave the womb. For most of us it happens gradually. We look in the mirror and see new wrinkles, new gray hairs, or a receding hairline. We have less stamina in our work. We get out of breath more easily going upstairs or carrying bundles or a suitcase. Cold and damp weather brings new or more frequent aches and twinges of pain. But we do not suddenly wake up one day to find ourselves *old*.

Perhaps one reason we fear aging is the idea of becoming physically ugly to others and being shunned by them. In our hearts we know physical beauty is not really important, and we love many people who are not externally attractive. But we are constantly bombarded with media statements about the importance of youth and beauty, and we are insecure enough at times to be taken in by them.

A few weeks ago I visited an older couple I have known for only a short time. They showed me snapshots of themselves taken twenty years ago on a trip. At first I failed to recognize the attractive young woman with a model's poise and the dapper young man with the mischievous grin in the pictures. They are still attractive people, but as I studied their earlier images, I thought how different they looked and how no one could have foretold the way they would change in appearance.

Visible aging affects our physical movements as well as appearance. A dancer spoke to me of her perception of her own aging. "I can still do the large movements, but I can't maintain the finer details consistently." The she whispered almost to herself, "I can see parts of myself floating away, and I'll never have them again." In a less vivid way each of us experiences our loss of ease in body movement as we age.

Another fear we might connect with aging is the fear of being avoided by others. If we did not know our grandparents we may have no loving memories of the elderly members of our family. We may not be attracted to the old, and so we fear no one will want to associate with us in our later years. Or we may have known elderly people who constantly criticized or complained or contradicted others. We saw how they were absorbed in their health or their problems and wished to talk about nothing else. As a result they were shunned by others.

When we face our own aging we must also face the fear that we will have no one to take care of us. Parents cannot be sure their adult children will have the means to support them. Older members of religious orders see fewer young men and women on whom they will be able to depend for spiritual and financial help as they grow less active.

When the sisters of my province gather, I see a group of vibrant, talented, but aging women. The median age of the province continues to rise. Who will take care of us when we need help? Where will we go? All of us must live with this uncertain future.

The experience of growing older

My visible aging is a sign that my strength too is ebbing, that my body is not renewing itself so quickly as it used to. I am growing nearer to a time when I may be helpless, unable to take care of myself. One morning when I was unusually tired I spilled a bowl of cereal and started to cry. "I spilled my cereal," I wailed. I knew the matter was not serious, but deep inside was a feeling of helplessness and dread. I realize now that I felt my mortality at that moment. Unconsciously I feared old age when such an accident might happen more often. I do not want to be old and helpless, with or without pain. Today, even while we see that the elderly with the right diet and moderate exercise can stay active longer, we also see the onslaught of Alzheimer's and other debilitating diseases. Being helpless or in pain is not a necessary condition of the old, but we do associate these experiences with age.

One of the greatest fears connected with aging is the loss of family and friends through death. When our parents, aunts, and uncles die, we see ourselves becoming the buffer generation, the one between death and the next generation. But we expect people older than we are to die. It is when our contemporaries begin to go that we experience another kind of loneliness. Those who have lived through special moments with us cannot be replaced. Young people, with all the good will in the world, cannot share experiences common to my generation, cannot feel nostalgia for what they have never known, cannot share in my generation's special memories.

When we lose someone special with whom we have shared at a deep and vulnerable level, we lose a friend we cannot replace. The process of making friends takes time, and as we grow older, we see time moving by us more and more rapidly. Just as one cannot age a choice wine quickly, so one cannot force a friendship. And yet time is just what we have less of.

The thought of less time is frightening in itself. We have less and less time to make our mark on the world, to satisfy our desire for what Carl Jung describes as generativity, to leave behind some part of ourselves to live on in the world as a memorial. The book not yet written, the students not yet taught, the memories not yet created with others—all need more time than we have left. We do not want to be forgotten, yet we know how quickly older people who have gone before us have been forgotten. Perhaps we envy our sisters and brothers who have their children and grandchildren as their legacy to the world. We may not regret our own choice of a celibate life, but as we see time speeding by our panic increases to produce "something worthwhile" with our lives.

Other hopes are constricted by time. Estrangements are not resolved, and the hope that they will be healed weakens as the bitterness settles in and reconciliation seems less likely. Family members fear death will intervene while brother and sister continue to refuse to speak to each other. Formerly close friends decline to be the first to break the barrier of silence. And time passes.

Perhaps the greatest fear we associate with aging is that we will be useless. So many of us grew up equating our self-worth with our productivity and our success in work. As long as we are bringing in a paycheck, contributing something to the group or family, we are worthwhile. When we are sick or retired, we fear we will be a burden to others.

We all know people who stayed at their work longer than they should have. They became a joke to their students or a source of frustration to their colleagues. Sometimes the fault lay with superiors and administrators who left aging religious in a position because there was no one else to take their place. But sometimes the religious chose to stay on in their work because they feared retirement as a time of isolation and boredom. "I don't want to go to the retirement home and sit in a rocking chair all day."

Guidelines for coping

How do we deal with these fears of aging? The first and most important step is to face our fears, to name and express them. We will find we are not alone in our fears; we share them with almost every one else. Over a century ago the poet William Cullen Bryant suggested in "Thanatopsis" that realizing we share a common fate with others can be a comfort in facing the fear of aging and death.

> Yet not to thine eternal resting-place
> Shalt thou retire alone. . . . Thou shalt lie down
> With patriarchs of the infant world—with kings,
> The powerful of the earth—the wise, the good,
> Fair forms, and hoary seers of ages past,
> All in one mighty sepulchre.[1]

The cycle of nature shows us the richness that comes with aging: the autumn harvest is the colorful maturity of spring's buds in the fruit we enjoy. We see this same harvest in the productivity of older artists from Michelangelo to Grandma Moses, in the contribution to the world of great elders from Albert Einstein to Pope John XXIII to Dorothy Day. Their biographies can convince us that old age is not a barrier to happy productive years. In the arts, we see the mature talent and technique in the work actors, artists, and musicians produced in the second half of their lives. For instance, Rembrandt's self-portraits are rich studies in the process of aging. To look at them carefully one by one is to see a man gradually worn by care and time, but growing old with dignity. He is not handsome, but the tolerance and understanding etched in his face draw us to him.

Loving ourselves

Sometimes our feverish activity prevents us from admitting our fear that if we knew ourselves better we would not like ourselves. Perhaps we need to slow down our activities and spend some time getting to know the person we really are. If our fear of aging suggests to us that we will have more time to be alone with ourselves in the years ahead, then we had better be sure we like the person with whom we will be spending that time.

How many times have we heard, "If people really knew me, they might not like me." Living with this attitude is painful and lonely, as many of us know from experience. A basic requirement for a happy life at any age is sincere self-love. If we do not yet love ourselves as we are with our weak points and warts, we have a vital lesson to learn as we age more visibly.

Self-image is a problem for many of us. No matter how loving the family in which we were raised, we experience nagging insecurities at times. If there were problems in the home, the effects may still be with us. An alcoholic, absent, or critical parent may have chipped away at our self-esteem. The competition in school, peer or sibling rivalry, lack of support, all can leave us with weakened self-love. If we once thought we were valued for what we did rather than what we were, we may still equate our self-worth with our performance. Thus a failure in work is a failure as a person.

Christ told us to love others as ourselves. In this sense, self-love is essential. If we are not lovable in our own eyes, we will not believe that anyone else loves us, even God. When we love ourselves we can acknowledge our faults and imperfections and admit our shortcomings. They are only part of us, a part that can change. The person we *are,* created by God with rich potential, is a lovable human being. We must not confuse our mistakes and weaknesses with the essence of who we are.

Most of us are gentle with the faults of others. We should be no less gentle with ourselves. "God hates the sin, but loves the sinner." We are not merely our weak-willed behavior, our procrastination, our spirit of envy or revenge. We have our strengths and gifts as well. If we are honest with ourselves, we will embrace both the positive and negative aspects of our character as we grow in love for ourselves.

In these last few paragraphs I have not attempted a detailed program for building up one's self-image. But as I have indicated, we can be as forgiving of ourselves as we are of others, look around us and realize that no one is perfect, and open ourselves to being vulnerable. Baring our soul to casual strangers is unwise, but we can show ourselves as we are to a few carefully chosen people. We can build up our confidence and trust slowly, just as they were once eroded.

Sometimes the way we present ourselves to others dictates the way they will treat us. A reporter experimented by disguising herself as an old woman and timidly asking a store clerk to help her find a certain item. The clerk dismissed her with a wave of his hand in the general direction of the shelves where the item was located. Later the reporter went back to the store as her own assertive self, and the clerk not only accompanied her to the shelves but took time to explain the item's proper use. Most of us need a course in assertiveness training to find the balance between respecting the rights of others and having our own respected.

Recently in a grocery store I witnessed a conversation between an elderly person, partly deaf and blind, and the clerk at the meat counter. The woman knew exactly which cut of meat she wanted. At first the clerk did not take her seriously. But the elderly woman handled the interaction with the clerk in such an assured and dignified way that he finally went out back and cut some meat to her specifications. The clerk's expression during their exchange was interesting to watch: at first a little amused, a little dubious, but finally respectful as one equal to another. The incident strengthened my belief that whatever our age, the way we present ourselves affects the way others treat us.

Broadening our world

Another way to prepare for aging is to broaden our world now. If all our activities and friendships are bound up in our work, we will fear aging and retirement much more than if some of our interests are outside of work. If we need youthful stamina and reflexes for our hobbies and leisure interests, we will be at a loss to enjoy our free time when we are physically less strong.

The first way to widen our horizon is to read about old age and retirement, so we will know what to expect as the years pass. Research into the facts about aging can dispel some of the myths we now believe. We will find that mental impairment is not inevitable, and serious visual and hearing impairments are only slightly more common among the elderly. Persons over sixty-five are not too rigid to learn, although they may be more inclined to solve problems on the basis of past solutions rather than experiment with new ones. A large proportion of the elderly are not isolated from their families and other social relationships nor are they institutionalized. The elderly display great differences within the same age group as people do at any age; but on the whole, their creative abilities and activities continue. While most older people experience a decline in functioning, they generally learn to compensate for these declines as do younger people who lose a limb or a sense such as sight. The majority of older people retain basic health at least through their sixties. Many times a decline in mental functioning is only apparent under stressful conditions.

Since aging begins at conception, it is a continuous but slow process. Different parts of the human body develop and decline at different rates. Aging is not a disease. It is a normal process. Learning the facts about aging can give us the courage to face its realities without despair or pessimistic fatalism.

As our bodies age, they need more time to renew themselves when we make unusual demands on them. If we are sensitive to their warnings of over-exertion, we will find that they serve us well. With a good working schedule, a well-balanced nutritious diet, and prudent regular exercise, we can enjoy a normal lifestyle well into our senior years. Adequate care naturally includes an annual physical examination and attention to any unusual physical changes in our bodies.

Some of our fears about aging concern events or conditions that are not restricted to aging. If God has given us good health with which to enjoy life up to this point, then we can certainly trust for the future. If on the other hand we have suffered poor health, then we can trust that future burdens will never be more than we can bear. As I mentioned earlier, if we develop a proper sense of our self-worth, we will not feel useless because we are unable to work.

Our minds have an important effect on our physical well-being. A positive attitude to the inevitable ups and downs of our daily life will prevent undue stress. Learning to face problems in a practical way without making a crisis of every one is also important. Whatever we learn now that helps us deal with daily difficulties will not only increase our happiness in the present but serve as an investment in our future. In this way we will become more serene in our aging process.

Reading and attending lectures can help us to know ourselves better. Whether we choose to learn about the enneagram or the Myers-Briggs Type Indicator or experiment with different kinds of prayer, we learn to understand ourselves better and become more interesting persons, even to ourselves. Sometimes in the course of our reading or a workshop, we may find a piece of knowledge that lights up a past experience, helping us to see meaning where we saw none before. Suddenly we understand why that person reacted the way she did, or why we find a certain interaction difficult. Such knowledge can help us come to terms with the past and heal some of the hurts we still carry with us.

Seeking this type of knowledge is healthy because experts in adult development agree that problems not addressed during life's earlier transitions or in the midlife crisis will surface again in later years, sometimes with renewed vigor. Dealing with them then is much more difficult than if we had done so at an earlier age. Other problems may even have built upon them.

Sometimes in the past we were not free to make choices. We had responsibilities; we had made commitments. Aging, the sensation that time is passing, can encourage us to make a necessary change in our lifestyle or to begin to use a talent or ability that we had not recognized before. One art critic suggested that when Grandma Moses began painting, her style was fairly traditional. But her failing eyesight led her to choose bright colors and produced her primitive style of painting which proved to be so popular. For her a physical impairment helped her creative process.

In preparing for retirement we need to develop interests that we can continue into our senior years. Reading and writing are two pleasures I expect to enjoy indefinitely. We can experiment with arts and crafts or music to express our love of beauty. Gardening is a holistic hobby; when we lavish care on plants, they respond with beauty. In addition, when our minds are absorbed with the plants, we forget our other worries. If our interests at present are not suitable for later years, we need to develop new ones. We will not suddenly acquire new interests on our fiftieth or sixtieth birthday.

Many people think first of monetary matters when they think of their old age. None of us can be sure of financial security in our last years, but to spend the present worrying about the future is not wise. I once worked with a middle-aged woman who was unhappy in her job. She felt she could not leave it because she had too much invested in the retirement pension plan, and she would lose a good part of the money if she left before she retired. A few months after we talked about this problem, she drowned in a boating accident. I regret that she had not sought more enjoyable work years earlier, rather than remain in a position where she was unhappy, for the sake of an uncertain retirement. Surely the quality of life is as important as the quantity. Rather than be anxious about the future, we can plan for it to the best of our ability with the knowledge and resources we have, and trust God for the rest.

Role models

In this process of aging we need to look for role models. I can think of two women religious who grew old gracefully. One woman lived in pre-Vatican II days, yet within the narrow structures of the time, she showed a breadth of view and a compassion that warmed all who knew her. As a secondary school principal she was a grandmotherly figure to the students, loving yet firm. Her talks over the sound system instilled such a sense of pride in the students that I could see them sitting up a little straighter as she spoke.

The other woman is in her eighties now, still gracious and generous. She spends a few hours each day tutoring students, engages in social justice activities such as writing letters about important legislation to members of Congress, and takes her turn to prepare the community's evening meal. She is fortunate to have her health, but she has also cut back on more strenuous activities so she is not draining her energies. Thus she is able to live a happy productive life.

My father was also a role model for me in the process of aging. When he retired from the army, he could have continued in the same position as a civilian, but he chose to do odd jobs that he enjoyed. He helped a friend paint his house, gardened, made improvements around his own home, and travelled to visit friends. I remember sitting with him in the back yard after his last illness began. As he watched his only granddaughter playing he said, "It's been a good life. If I had it to live over again I'd do it the same way. I have no regrets." I hope I will be able to make the same statement as I approach death.

Some of the problems we may associate with aging can occur at any age. Complaining and critical attitudes are not necessarily attributes of the later years. We all know young cynics and critics who are rigid and judgmental, young people with no sense of humor and no ability to adapt to others. Nor do the elderly have a monopoly on loneliness. We know that at any age we can be with a crowd of people, and if there is no one there to whom we are drawn or who seems to take an interest in us, we can feel terribly alone. One friend remarked to me that she knows of nothing worse than to be present in a group of people who probably consider themselves her friends, and to find herself thinking, "I have nothing in common with these men and women." Loneliness like so many other human emotions is not something we can escape, but we can use it for our own growth.[2]

A bright future

Grow old along with me!
The best is yet to be,
The last of life, for which the first was made.[3]

The first time I read these lines I smiled at the poet's romanticized view of aging. But as I reflected on the words, I had to admit that I would never want to be a teenager again. When I remember the "crises" that rocked my life in those years, the turmoil, the insecurity, I feel no nostalgia. I worried how I would score on tests. I prayed that my complexion would clear by Friday. My highs and lows depended on my peers. I agonized over who liked me or what impression I had made on a new acquaintance or when my appearance would begin to resemble my ideal. I can look back now to each decade of my life and see how I have grown, learned new skills, developed self-confidence, become more the person I want to be. I know that I am growing better as I age and I hope I will continue to improve until the day I die. This process is so much better than starting out perfect in youth and going progressively down hill!

One of nature's hardest laws is the survival of the fittest. When I pass by a woods and see the small misshapen trees that have been crowded out by the bigger ones, and the odd shapes and lack of lower branches on some trees that have grown to a striking height, I feel pity for them. Yet survival, life, is a precious gift. The elderly are survivors: they have their scars, it is true, but many have also their humor and their wisdom.

When I was growing up my favorite tree was an old gnarled apple tree. Some of its branches touched the ground, and all of them grew in odd curves and shapes, perfect for climbing and sitting in and leaning against while I pretended or daydreamed. If that tree had grown tall and straight toward the sky, I might have admired and respected it, but I would not have loved it and spent time close to it the way I did. And so survival does not have to be a gloomy word. It is good to be a survivor. If we are ready for retirement, then we have survived till now and we are strong. If we are looking ahead to retirement, then we are the stuff of which survivors are made. In either case, we are fortunate.

The most important preparation for aging and retirement is to intensify our spiritual life. Aging brings inevitable losses and limitations. We learn to live without those we loved and with whom we shared so much. We compensate for increasing physical disabilities. We relinquish our youthful dreams. As life detaches us from our absorption with the things of this world, aging is a natural prelude to thoughts of death. We need a rich prayer life to appreciate the importance of spiritual values as we draw nearer to facing our Creator.[4]

I remember seeing a small child crying for a red pencil her mother was using. All around her on the floor were toys with which she had been playing, but at that moment the only object she had set her heart on was her mother's pencil. As we grow older we see more clearly that our lives are full of red pencils that we do not need. Reflecting on our past experiences, we recognize that painful detachments only freed us to be more truly ourselves. Our own journey probably reflects Jung's belief that the second half of life is a search for the spiritual. This letting go of ceaseless striving after possessions, status, honor, none of which we take with us beyond the grave, is a prelude to peace. Realizing the unimportance of these transitory goals, we place more emphasis on eternal and spiritual values.

One of the most appropriate gospel scenes for us to reflect on is the story of the disciples who met Christ on the way to Emmaus. They were discouraged and afraid as they walked along. When a stranger joined them, they were amazed he did not know of the disastrous death of their hopes in Jerusalem. But then as the stranger reviewed scripture with them, they began to see some meaning behind the events. They asked the stranger to join them, "Stay with us for it is now toward evening," and then they recognized Jesus in the breaking of the bread (Luke 24:13-31).

Let us make this prayer our own. "Stay with me, Lord, for I am growing toward the evening of my life." Whatever our age, let us build on the past and nourish the seeds of the future within us. May we continue to grow in wisdom and grace as we move toward the evening shadows and our own resurrection encounter with Christ.

> There is great beauty in old trees
> Old streets and ruins old
> Why should not I as well as these
> Grow lovely growing old?[5]

Endnotes

1. William Cullen Bryant, "Thanatopsis," in *The Poetical Works of William Cullen Bryant,* Parke Godwin, ed., vol. 1 (New York: Russell and Russell, 1967 [1883]), p. 18.

2. Sr. Anna Polcino, M.D., F.A.P.A., has written a helpful article on how to use loneliness to grow closer to God. See *Loneliness: The Genesis of Solitude, Friendship, and Contemplation* (Whitinsville, Mass.: Affirmation Books, 1979).

3. Robert Browning, "Rabbi Ben Ezra," in *The Complete Poetic and Dramatic Works of Robert Browning* (Boston: Houghton Mifflin, 1895), p. 383.

4. See Kathleen Fischer, *Winter Grace* (New York: Paulist Press, 1985) for a discussion of spirituality for the later years.

5. Inscription on a tombstone in St. Just-in-Roseland churchyard, Cornwall, England. See Book of Job 12:12.

Affirmation Books is an important part of the ministry of the House of Affirmation, International Therapeutic Center for Clergy and Religious, founded by Sr. Anna Polcino, M.D., F.A.P.A., and Fr. Thomas A. Kane, Ph.D., D.P.S. Income from the sale of Affirmation books and tapes is used to provide care for priests and religious suffering from emotional unrest.

The House of Affirmation provides a threefold program of service, education, and research. Among its services are five residential therapeutic communities and three counseling centers in the United States and one residential center in England. All centers provide nonresidential counseling. The House sponsors a leadership conference each year during the first week of February and a month-long Institute of Applied Psychotheology during July. More than forty clinical staff members conduct workshops and symposiums throughout the year.

For further information, write or call the administrative offices in Boston, Massachusetts.

The House of Affirmation
22 The Fenway
Boston, Massachusetts 02215
617/266-8792